SCANDI
BITES

SCANDI BITES

60 recipes for sweet treats, party food and other little Scandinavian snacks

Trine Hahnemann

Photography by Columbus Leth
Illustrations by Debbie Powell

Hardie Grant

QUADRILLE

Contents

Introduction

Scandinavia is the land of *hygge*, *fika* or the *kaffepause* – any excuse to take a break. Having coffee with cakes and treats is part of daily life, be it at home or in a café. Scandinavians like buns and pastries in the morning, sandwiches for lunch and snacks during the day, and cakes in the afternoon. This tradition is perfect for someone like me who never seems to fall out of love with baking.

When I grew up, we had three main meals a day and some treats in between. Times are changing, and we eat more fluidly during the day now; often it is more about small bites throughout the day than about major meals. Then buns, crispbread or just a slice of rye bread with a topping are great choices: easy to eat and light, but most importantly tasty.

Home baking is still something I love to do, and even though I now own the bakery in Copenhagen, Hahnemanns Køkken, I still bake at home – my rye bread, buns and a

cake now and then. It means a lot to me; I really enjoy roaming around my kitchen and I often do more than one thing while baking, like listening to a podcast or writing and drinking endless cups of tea. It is a way for me to relax, in my favourite room in my house – the kitchen.

This book is a collection of some of my favourite things to eat. You could say that it is my treasure trove of Scandi bites, recipes that I keep revisiting – some frequently and others mostly in the holiday season. I might forget about them but one of them re-emerges again a while later and I get all excited about cooking it again, as if I were seeing an old friend.

Consider this book a small window into the Scandi way of eating and get inspired to make some of the things I eat and make. Remember always to embrace the act of baking, not just the end result of eating; both the process and the time spent at the dining table are a part of life's joy.

Fika + Teatime

Cinnamon buns

<<<<<<<<<<<<<<<<<<<<<<<<<<<<<<<<<<<<<<<<<<<<<<<<<<<<<<<<<<<<<<<<<<<<<<<<<<<<<<<

Makes 18–20

For the buns
50g/2oz fresh yeast
500ml/2 cups lukewarm
  whole milk
1 egg, lightly beaten
850g/7 cups 00 grade (tipo 00)
  flour, plus more to dust
100g/½ cup caster or
  granulated sugar
2 tsp ground cardamom
½ tsp salt
150g/⅔ cup soft butter
For the filling
200g/⅞ cup soft butter
150g/1¼ cups caster or
  granulated sugar
4 tsp ground cinnamon

You can make the dough and leave it to rise in the refrigerator for 1 or 2 days. I never have time, because there are always some impatient children waiting...

Crumble the yeast into the milk and stir to dissolve, then add the egg. Now mix in the flour, sugar, cardamom and salt. Mix the butter into the dough, then knead well on a floured work surface. Put the dough into a bowl, cover with a tea towel and let it rise in a warm place for one or two hours, or until doubled in size.

Make the filling by mixing together the butter, sugar and cinnamon. Divide the dough in half and roll each piece out on a floured work surface to make a rectangle measuring about 40 x 30cm/16 x 12in. Spread the cinnamon filling over each. Roll each piece of dough into a wide cylinder, starting from a long side to get a long, slim log, then cut into 2.5cm/1in slices.

Line some baking sheets with baking parchment. Place the cinnamon rolls on the paper, pressing down on each one so they spread slightly. Cover and leave to rise again, in a warm place, for 30 minutes.

Preheat the oven to 180°C/350°F/gas mark 4. Bake the cinnamon buns for 25–30 minutes. Leave to cool on a wire rack before serving.

◇◇◇

There are countless recipes for these famous buns. I think they have to be soft, with a crisp shell, and that there has be cardamom in the dough. Also, the mixture has to have the right balance of spice and sweet.

◇◇◇

There's a legendary Scandi children's story called *When the Robbers Came to Cardamom Town* about some rather nice robbers... Why Cardamom town, I don't know... I suppose it just shows how much we love cardamom!

Cardamom knots

<<<<<<<<<<<<<<<<<<<<<<<<<<<<<<<<<<<<<<<<<<<<<<<<<<<<<<<<<<<<<<<<

Makes 18–20

For the filling
200g/⅞ cup soft butter
150g/1¼ cups caster or
   granulated sugar
2 tsp ground cardamom
For the knutar
1 quantity Cinnamon buns
   dough (see page 12)
00 grade (tipo 00), or plain/
   all-purpose flour, to dust
1 egg, lightly beaten

Make the filling by mixing together the butter, sugar and cardamom.

Divide the dough in half and roll each piece out on a floured work surface to make a 40 x 30cm/16 x 12in rectangle. Spread the cardamom filling lengthways over half of each rectangle. Fold the plain side over the filled, then cut crossways into 2cm/¾in strips. Roll these strips of dough twice round your hand, then secure with the end, pulling it through the middle of the mass as you would a hank of leftover wool (this forms the 'knot' shape). Place on baking sheets lined with baking parchment. Cover with tea towels and leave to rise in a warm place for 30 minutes.

Preheat the oven to 180°C/350°F/gas mark 4.

Brush with the egg and bake for 20–25 minutes, then leave the knots to cool on a wire rack.

Buttermilk buns

◇◇

Makes 12
―――――

For the buns
50g/2oz fresh yeast
200ml/⅞ cup buttermilk
1 egg, lightly beaten
300g/2½ cups 00 grade (tipo 00)
  flour, plus more to dust
75g/⅜ cup caster or
  granulated sugar
1 tsp salt
100g/scant ½ cup cold butter
For the filling
150g/5¼oz good marzipan
  (page 136), coarsely grated
100g/scant ½ cup soft butter
2 Tbsp caster/superfine sugar
For the topping
1 egg, lightly beaten
100g/¾ cup skin-on almonds,
  finely chopped

Crumble the yeast into the buttermilk and stir to dissolve, then stir in the egg. In a separate bowl, mix the flour, sugar and salt. Cut the butter into cubes and rub it into the flour with your fingers until it looks like crumbs. Stir in the yeast mixture, then knead the dough on a floured work surface until smooth. Return the dough to the bowl, cover with a tea towel and leave to rise in a warm place for one hour.

Mix together all the ingredients for the filling.

Roll out the dough into a circle on a floured work surface, spread the filling evenly over it, then cut into 12 triangles. Roll each into a little horn (kind of similar to a croissant but without the curve, see photo, right) and place on baking sheets lined with baking parchment. Leave to rise again, in a warm place, for 30 minutes.

Preheat the oven to 200°C/400°F/gas mark 6. Brush the pastries with the egg, sprinkle with the almonds and bake for 20–25 minutes. Leave to cool on a wire rack.

◇◇

This is an old-fashioned type of pastry that young people do not really know. But they can bring tears to older generations, who remember their mothers baking them.

◇◇

◇◇◇◇◇◇◇◇◇◇◇◇◇◇◇◇◇◇◇◇◇◇◇

Frøsnappe, we call these. They are perfect for morning coffee or brunch, though I can easily eat one heated up, late at night, with a cup of strong tea.

◇◇◇◇◇◇◇◇◇◇◇◇◇◇◇◇◇◇◇◇◇◇◇

Poppy and sesame seed Danish

<<<<<<<<<<<<<<<<<<<<<<<<<<<<<<<<<<<<<<<<<<<<<<<<<<<<<<<<<<<<<<<<<<<<<<>

Makes about 20

For the filling
150g/⅔ cup butter
5 Tbsp caster or
   granulated sugar
50g/1¾oz poppy seeds
For the rest
1 quantity Basic Danish pastry
   dough (see page 132)
00 grade (tipo 00), or plain/
   all-purpose flour, to dust
1 egg, lightly beaten
100g/¾ cup poppy seeds
100g/¾ cup sesame seeds

Mix the butter and sugar for the filling together with the poppy seeds.

Roll the Danish pastry dough out on a lightly floured work surface to a 60 x 30cm/24 x 12in rectangle. Spread the filling, lengthways, on one half of the dough, then fold the plain half of the dough over the filling: the folded pastry should measure 60 x 15cm/24 x 6in. Press the seams together to encase it and brush with egg (reserve the remaining egg), then dredge with the poppy seeds and sesame seeds for the topping so the dough is covered.

Cut the pastry crossways into long strips, each 15 x 4cm/6 x 1½in. Take one at a time, twist them, then place on a baking sheet lined with baking parchment. Cover with tea towels and leave to rest in a warm place for 30 minutes.

Preheat the oven to 220°C/425°F/gas mark 7.

Brush each pastry with the reserved egg on the cut edges and the pieces that aren't covered with seeds, so every bit turns golden in the oven, then bake for 5 minutes. Reduce the oven temperature to 200°C/400°F/gas mark 6 and bake for 15 minutes. Leave to cool on a wire rack.

19

Poppy seed Danish

<<<<<<<<<<<<<<<<<<<<<<<<<<<<<<<<<<<<<<<<<<<<<<<<<<<<<<<<<<<<<<<<

Makes 18

For the dough
25g/generous ¾oz fresh yeast
150ml/⅔ cup lukewarm water
1 egg, lightly beaten, plus an
  extra beaten egg to glaze
1 tsp salt
½ tsp ground cardamom
1 Tbsp caster or
  granulated sugar
325g/2¾ cups 00 grade (tipo
  00) flour, plus extra for dusting
300g/1⅓ cups cold butter,
  thinly sliced
For the filling
75g/⅓ cup soft butter
75g/scant ½ cup caster or
  granulated sugar
100g/3½oz raisins, chopped
75g/2½oz poppy seeds

Crumble the yeast into the water, stir to dissolve, then add the egg, salt, cardamom and sugar. Stir in the flour and knead the dough with your hands until it is even and combined. Put it in a bowl, cover with cling film/plastic wrap and leave to rest in the fridge for about 15 minutes.

Roll out the dough on a lightly floured surface into roughly a 45-cm/18-in square. Arrange the butter slices in a square in the centre of the dough, at a 45-degree angle to the corners of the dough so it forms a smaller diamond inside the dough square. Fold the corners of the dough over the butter to encase it fully and seal the joins well. Roll out the dough again carefully, this time into a rectangle, making sure that it does not crack and expose the butter.

Fold a short end one-third over into the centre, and the other short end over that, as you would a business letter. Wrap in cling film and rest again in the fridge for 15 minutes. Repeat this rolling and folding procedure 3 times in total, remembering to let the dough rest for 15 minutes in the fridge between each.

Now make the filling. Mix the ingredients together until combined. Line 2 baking sheets with baking parchment.

Roll out the dough on a floured surface to a rectangle about 60 x 40cm/24 x 16in. Spread the filling evenly over the dough and, with the longest side facing you, roll it up like a Swiss roll. Cut the roll into 1.5-cm/¹/₂-in pieces and place, cut side up, on the lined baking sheets. Cover with tea towels and let them rise for 30 minutes. Preheat the oven to 220°C/425°F/gas mark 7.

Brush the snails with beaten egg and bake in the oven for 15–18 minutes.

◇◇◇

If you go to a bakery in Denmark and ask for a snail, you will get
a Danish with a swirl of cinnamon filling. I can't get enough of poppy
seeds, so I make poppy seed swirls instead. This is perfect in my world.

◇◇◇

Jam or pastry cream Danish

<><><><><><><><><><><><><><><><><><><><><><><><><><><><><><><><><><><><><><><><><><><><><><><><><><>

Makes 24

1 quantity Basic Danish pastry
   dough (see page 132)
00 grade (tipo 00), or plain/
   all-purpose flour, to dust
½ quantity Pastry Cream
   (see page 27)
100g/3½oz jam of your choice
1 egg, lightly beaten

Roll out the Danish pastry dough on a lightly floured work surface to 60 x 40cm/24 x 16in and cut out 10-cm/4-in squares. Place 1–2 tsp of either Pastry Cream or jam in the middle of each square, so you have 12 of each variety.

Now form the pastries: take each square and fold the corners into the middle over the cream until all 4 meet. Close all the dough seams by pressing them together so the cream is encased (it doesn't matter, on this occasion, if you don't seal them completely). Place on baking sheets lined with baking parchment, cover with tea towels and leave to rest in a warm place for 30 minutes.

Preheat the oven to 220°C/425°F/gas mark 7. Brush the pastries with the egg and bake for 5 minutes, then reduce the oven temperature to 200°C/400°F/gas mark 6 and bake for 15 minutes. They will have opened up like the petals of a flower, to reveal the filling within.

Leave to cool on a wire rack.

This *Spandau* pastry divides the Scandinavians: jam or pastry cream?
You get to choose here, as I have given you both, equally delicious options.

Marzipan and poppy seed Danish

Makes 20

150g/5¼oz good marzipan (page 136), coarsely grated
125g/generous ½ cup soft butter
3 Tbsp caster or granulated sugar
1 quantity Basic Danish pastry dough (see page 132)
00 grade (tipo 00), or plain/all-purpose flour, to dust
1 egg, lightly beaten
50–100g/⅓–⅔ cup poppy seeds

Mix the marzipan, butter and sugar together to make a smooth paste and set aside at room temperature.

Roll out the Danish pastry dough on a lightly floured work surface to 56 x 36cm/22 x 14in then cut it in half lengthways. Roll both out a little more until you have a pair of equal rectangles, each measuring 60 x 18cm/24 x 7½in.

Halve the marzipan filling. Take 1 portion and spread it evenly, lengthways, on one half of a dough rectangle. Fold the plain half over the marzipan half to give a filled pastry measuring 60 x 9cm/24 x 3½in. Repeat with the other dough rectangle. Push the seams of the dough gently together. Brush both with the egg (reserve the remaining egg) and dredge with poppy seeds. Cut crossways into 5-cm/2-in pieces and place them on baking sheets lined with baking parchment. Cover with a tea towel and leave to rest in a warm place for 30 minutes.

Preheat the oven to 220°C/425°F/gas mark 7.

Brush each pastry with reserved egg on the cut sides, so they turn brown. Bake for 5 minutes, then reduce the oven temperature to 200°C/400°F/gas mark 6 and bake for another 15 minutes. Leave to cool on a wire rack.

◇◇◇◇◇◇◇◇◇◇◇◇◇◇◇◇◇◇◇◇◇

At the weekend the traditional Scandinavian breakfast is rolls, cheese, butter and jam, your favourite Danish and – of course – filter coffee. This recipe is very much a Copenhagen thing. Just 100km away, where my family is from on the Island of Fyn, they call this pastry a *Københavner*, meaning somebody from Copenhagen. I still find it fascinating that in such a small country there can be so many regional variations. You can leave the marzipan out of the filling here, if you prefer.

◇◇◇◇◇◇◇◇◇◇◇◇◇◇◇◇◇◇◇◇◇

◇◇◇

This pastry is the one I bake for a family birthday breakfast table. This has become an important tradition; I started doing it when I became a mother, when I lived in London and could not find proper *wienerbrød* anywhere.

◇◇◇

Chocolate Danish

<<<<<<<<<<<<<<<<<<<<<<<<<<<<<<<<<<<<<<<<<<<<<<<<<<<<<<<<<<<<<<<<

Makes 24

___

For the pastry cream
300ml/1¼ cups single/light
cream
1 vanilla pod/bean, split
lengthways
3 egg yolks, plus 1 whole egg,
lightly beaten, to glaze
3 Tbsp caster or granulated
sugar
1 Tbsp cornflour/cornstarch
For the rest
1 quantity Basic Danish pastry
dough (see page 132)
00 grade (tipo 00), or plain/
all-purpose flour, to dust
200g/7oz best dark chocolate,
at least 60% cocoa solids,
chopped
20g/1½ Tbsp butter

Bring the cream to the boil with the vanilla pod in a saucepan, then turn off the heat. In a bowl, whisk the egg yolks, sugar and cornflour together until fluffy and light yellow in colour. Pour a little bit of the hot cream into the egg mixture, whisking all the time, then pour all the egg mixture into the saucepan. Set the saucepan over a low heat and whisk until the cream starts to thicken. Take care not to boil and whisk continuously to avoid burning. When it has thickened, remove from the heat and leave to cool, placing a sheet of cling film/plastic wrap directly on the surface to prevent a skin forming.

Roll out the Danish pastry dough on a lightly floured work surface into a rectangle measuring 60 x 40cm/24 x 16in. Now cut it into 10-cm/4-in squares. Place 1–2 tsp of the pastry cream in the middle of each square.

Now form the pastries: take each square and fold the corners into the middle over the cream until all 4 meet. Close all the dough seams completely by pressing them together so the cream is encased. Now pull the new 4 'corners' of the dough up as well, to make a very tight ball of pastry around the cream. Turn each bun upside down, so it is smooth-side up, and place on a baking sheet lined with baking parchment. Cover with tea towels and leave to rest in a warm place for 30 minutes.

Preheat the oven to 220°C/425°F/gas mark 7. Brush the pastries with the egg to glaze and bake them for 15–18 minutes. Leave to cool on a wire rack.

Melt the chocolate in a heatproof bowl fitted over a saucepan of simmering water, making sure the bowl does not touch the water. Remove from the heat and stir in the butter, then leave to cool slightly. Spoon a little chocolate glaze on each pastry and spread it out with a spoon to a circle that stops 5mm/⅛in from the edge of the pastry. Leave the chocolate to set, then serve right away.

Spelt and anise rolls

<><><><><><><><><><><><><><><><><><><><><><><><><><><><><><><><><><><><><><><><><><><><><><><><>

Makes 25

50g/2oz fresh yeast
800ml/3⅓ cups lukewarm
 water
2 Tbsp honey
500g/4¼ cups wholegrain
 stoneground spelt flour
600g/5 cups white stoneground
 spelt flour, plus more to dust
2–3 Tbsp anise seeds, plus more
 for the top
1 tsp salt
1 egg, lightly beaten

Crumble the yeast into the lukewarm water to dissolve, then add the honey. In a separate bowl, mix the flours, anise and salt, add to the yeast mixture and stir until you have a smooth dough. Knead on a floured work surface, then return to the bowl, cover with a tea towel and leave to rise at room temperature for 2 hours.

Now form into 25 small rolls and place on baking sheets lined with baking parchment. Cover with a tea towel and leave to rise again, in a warm place, for 30 minutes. Preheat the oven to 200°C/400°F/gas mark 6.

Brush the rolls with the egg and sprinkle with anise seeds. Spray cold water in the oven to create steam and bake for 30 minutes, then cool on a wire rack.

The flavour of all forms of aniseed is much appreciated in Scandinavia, in sweets, alcohol and baking. It works perfectly in these breakfast buns, which taste great with Buttermilk Butter (page 131) and blackcurrant jam.

◇◇◇

Using up leftover bread goes back to a time when Scandinavia was a poor region and we simply could not afford food waste. There are many ways to turn bread into sweet things, and this is one of them.

◇◇◇

Coffee bread

<<<<<<<<<<<<<<<<<<<<<<<<<<<<<<<<<<<<<<<<<<<<<<<<<<<<<<<<<<<<<<

Makes 40

For the bread
50g/3½ Tbsp soft butter
400g/3⅓ cups strong white bread flour, plus extra for dusting
50g/⅓ cup caster or granulated sugar
2 tsp salt
25g/generous ¾oz fresh yeast
250ml/1 cup water
For the marzipan mixture
200g/7oz good marzipan (page 136)
300g/1½ cups caster or granulated sugar
3–4 organic egg whites
50g/6 Tbsp plain/all-purpose flour
½ tsp baking powder

Start by crumbling the butter into the flour in a mixing bowl, then stir in the sugar and salt. Dissolve the yeast in the water and add to the flour mixture, stirring to mix to a dough. Knead the dough well on a floured surface, return to the bowl, cover and leave to rise for 30 minutes.

Divide the dough in half and roll each half into a rectangle measuring about 12 x 34cm/4¾ x 13½in. Place both rectangles on a baking sheet lined with baking parchment and leave to rise for 1 hour. Preheat the oven to 180°C/350°F/gas mark 4.

Bake the bread for 20 minutes, then leave to cool on a wire rack. When cold, cut each rectangle into 20 slices and place on a wire rack with the cut side facing up. Toast in the oven until crisp, about 10 minutes.

While the bread slices are in the oven, grate the marzipan and mix with the sugar in a bowl. Add the egg whites a little at a time and whisk with a balloon whisk to a smooth mixture, then mix in the flour and baking powder. When the bread slices come out of the oven, spread the marzipan mixture onto each slice of bread, using a spoon or piping bag. Return to the oven and bake for 10–15 minutes or until golden brown. Leave to cool a little, then serve warm with a nice cup of coffee. Stored in an airtight container, they keep for a couple of weeks.

I have experimented a lot with making candy bars from dried fruit and have loved raw bars for years. This is my naturally vegan, gluten-free recipe that makes a great, healthy snack.

Raw bites

◇◇◇

Makes 30

140g/1 cup skin-on almonds
120g/1 cup raisins
275g/2 cups dates, stoned
50g/1¾oz coconut oil
50g/½ cup cacao powder
50ml/scant ¼ cup freshly
  squeezed orange juice
½ tsp pure vanilla powder or
  natural vanilla extract
1 tsp ground cinnamon
100g/3½oz desiccated/
  shredded coconut, to coat

Grind the almonds to a powder in a food processor.
    Add all the ingredients except the coconut to a food processor and process to a smooth paste. Remove from the processor and form into small squares by hand. You should get about 30 bars. Roll in the desiccated coconut to serve. They will keep in the refrigerator for 2–3 weeks.

In Scandinavia we eat a lot of bread with spices. Apart from cardamom in almost all soft sweet white bread, we also bake sweet rye bread with green anise. Called *limpa*, it's very common in Sweden, and when I go there I love going to a bakery to buy this distinctive tasting bread. I have been inspired by the flavours for years, and I bake different rolls and breads similar to the *limpa* bread.

Sweet rye rolls

<><><><><><><><><><><><><><><><><><><><><><><><><><><><><><><><><><><><><><><><><><>

Makes 24

Day 1
20g/¾oz fresh yeast
300ml/1¼ cups lukewarm water
125g/1 cup strong wholemeal
  bread flour

Day 2
600g/5 cups strong white bread
  flour, plus extra for dusting
200g/1⅔ cups wholegrain
  stoneground rye flour
50g/3½ Tbsp butter
2 tsp salt
10g/⅓oz anise seeds
50g/2oz fresh yeast
350ml/1½ cups lukewarm water
150g/5¼oz dark syrup (available
  from Scandinavian food sites,
  or replace with golden/corn
  syrup if necessary)
150g/1⅔ cups walnut halves
150g/1¼ cups dark raisins
1 egg, lightly beaten
50ml/scant ¼ cup cold coffee

Day 1
Crumble the yeast into the lukewarm water in a bowl and stir to dissolve. Mix in the wholemeal flour, cover with foil and leave overnight.

Day 2
The next day, mix the white and rye flours together in a bowl. Cut the butter into small cubes and rub it into the flours with your fingertips until it resembles crumbs. Add the salt. Roughly pound the anise seeds using a pestle and mortar, then add these as well.

In another bowl, crumble the yeast into the lukewarm water, then stir in the treacle and the flour and yeast mixture from the day before. Now mix this into the flour and butter mixture. Roughly chop the walnuts and add them to the bowl, with the raisins, and form into a smooth dough. Knead on a floured surface for 5 minutes.

Place in a big bowl, cover with cling film/plastic wrap and leave to rise for 2 hours. Knead lightly again and form into 24 rolls. Place on baking sheets lined with baking parchment, cover with tea towels and rise for 30 minutes. Meanwhile, preheat the oven to 200°C/400°F/gas mark 6.

Mix the egg with the coffee. Brush the rolls with some of the egg mixture. Spray cold water in the oven to create steam and bake for 5 minutes, then brush the loaves again with the coffee-egg wash, and bake for another 25–30 minutes. Leave to cool on a wire rack.

◇◇

I once asked my friend and author Carolyn Steel – whose family had been hoteliers – if she had a great shortcrust pastry recipe and her brother gave me this. It is now part of this classic Danish *linse* cake recipe with custard.

◇◇

Danish custard pies

<<<<<<<<<<<<<<<<<<<<<<<<<<<<<<<<<<<<<<<<<<<<<<<<<<<<<<<<<<<<<<<<<<<<<<<<<<<

Makes 12

For the pastry
110g/⅞ cup icing/confectioners'
   sugar
340g/2½ cups plain/
   all-purpose flour, plus more
   to dust
pinch of salt
225g/1 cup butter, chopped
1 egg, lightly beaten
For the custard
1 vanilla pod/bean
300ml/1¼ cups single/light
   cream
3 egg yolks
4 Tbsp caster or granulated
   sugar
1 Tbsp cornflour/cornstarch

Mix the icing sugar, flour and salt, then mix in the butter, either pulse-blending in a food processor or rubbing it in with your fingers, until the mixture has the consistency of crumbs. Add the egg and mix the dough until firm and smooth. Wrap in cling film/plastic wrap and let it rest in the refrigerator for 1 hour.

Meanwhile, make the custard. Split the vanilla pod lengthways. Heat the cream and vanilla pod in a saucepan until steaming hot, then turn off the heat. Whisk the egg yolks, sugar and cornflour together until fluffy and pale yellow. Pour a little of the hot cream into the egg mixture, then pour all the egg mixture into the saucepan. Set over a low heat and whisk until the custard starts to thicken. Take care not to boil the mixture and whisk continuously to avoid burning. Leave to cool completely.

Preheat the oven to 160°C/325°F/gas mark 3. Take the pastry out of the refrigerator and roll it out on a floured work surface to 5–8mm/¼–⅓in thick. Cut out rounds with a 7cm/2¾in cookie cutter and place them in a 12-hole fairy cake tin. Spoon in the custard. Roll out the remaining pastry and, with the same cookie cutter, cut out the lids. Place on top and press lightly around the edges. Bake for about 25 minutes or until golden brown. Leave to cool before serving. These will keep in an airtight container for 4 or 5 days.

Runeberg cakes

<><><><><><><><><><><><><><><><><><><><><><><><><><><><><><><><><><><><><><><><><><><><><><><><><><><><><><><><>

Makes 16 cakes

For the cakes
200g/⅞ cup butter
100g/½ cup soft brown sugar
100g/½ cup caster or
  granulated sugar
2 eggs
150g/1⅓ cups breadcrumbs
150g/1½ cups ground almonds
2 tsp baking powder
3 Tbsp finely grated organic
  orange zest
1 tsp ground cardamom
100g/7 Tbsp crème fraîche
150g/5¼oz Raspberry 'Jam'
  (page 138)

Preheat the oven to 180°C/350°F/gas mark 4. Cream the butter and sugars with an electric mixer until light and fluffy. Add the eggs one at a time, beating well after each addition.

Mix together the breadcrumbs, ground almonds and baking powder and fold into the cake batter with the orange zest, ground cardamom and crème fraîche. Pour half of it into a silicone canelle mould with 8 holes, filling each 1cm from the top. Bake for 30 minutes.

Let the Runeberg cakes cool down a bit before you take them out of the moulds. Place them on a wire rack to become completely cold while you bake the remaining 8 cakes in the same way.

Spoon the raspberry jam on the top of the cakes and serve, with whipped cream, if you like.

These cakes got their name from the Finnish poet Johan Ludvig Runeberg who, according to legend, enjoyed them every day for breakfast. They are very popular in Finland on the poet's birthday, 5 February.

Chocolate-topped medals

◇◇

Makes 10

For the pastry
200g/1½ cups plain/all-purpose flour, plus more to dust
50g/5 Tbsp icing/confectioners' sugar
1 tsp finely grated organic lemon zest
100g/scant ½ cup cold butter, chopped
½ egg, lightly beaten
For the apple compote
1 vanilla pod/bean
2 tart eating apples, such as Cox's Orange Pippin, peeled, cored and chopped
100g/½ cup caster or granulated sugar
For the cream and topping
200g/7oz best dark chocolate, at least 60% cocoa solids
20g/1½ Tbsp butter
200ml/⅞ cup double/heavy cream

To make the pastry, sift the flour and icing sugar into a bowl and add the lemon zest. Rub in the butter with your fingers until the mixture resembles crumbs. Add the egg and stir until the pastry comes together in a ball. Wrap in cling film/plastic wrap and chill for 30 minutes.

Meanwhile, for the filling, slit the vanilla pod in half lengthways and scrape out the seeds with the tip of a sharp knife. Put the apples in a saucepan with the sugar and the vanilla seeds and bring to the boil, then reduce the heat and leave to simmer for 20 minutes. Stir the apple mixture together to give a thick sauce, then leave to cool.

Preheat the oven to 220°C/425°F/gas mark 7. Line a baking sheet with baking parchment. Roll out the pastry on a floured work surface to a thickness of 2–3mm/¹⁄₁₆–⅛in. Use a 6–7cm/2½–2¾in diameter cookie cutter, or the rim of a similar-sized glass, to cut the pastry into about 20 discs (you will need an even number of discs, as you are going to be sandwiching them together). Spread them out on the lined baking sheet and bake for 6–7 minutes, then transfer carefully (they are a bit fragile) to a wire rack to cool.

continues >>

In Denmark, *medaljer* are usually offered for sale from bakeries in the afternoon, to be eaten with coffee, not tea. We Scandinavians are coffee-drinking nations. You can use any other fruit compote or jam instead of the apple compote here, if you prefer.

Meanwhile, break the chocolate for the topping into pieces, place in a small heatproof bowl with the butter and fit over a saucepan of simmering water; the bowl should not touch the water. When melted, leave to cool slightly. Spread half the discs with the chocolate mixture, leaving a slim border as in the photo. Set aside to let the chocolate set. These are the tops of the 'medals'.

Whip the cream until just stiff. Fit a piping bag with a 1cm/⅜in star-shaped nozzle and fill with whipped cream. Take the remaining pastry discs and place 1 tsp of apple sauce in the centre of each. Pipe a ring of cream around the apple sauce. Put the chocolate-coated medals on top and serve immediately.

Raspberry variation

For the pastry
See page 40
For the cream
200ml/⅞ cup double/heavy cream
150g/5½oz raspberries
2 Tbsp icing/confectioners' sugar
For the topping
100g/¾ cup icing/confectioners' sugar
2–3 Tbsp redcurrant jelly
2 handfuls of raspberries, to decorate

Make and bake the pastry medals as described on page 40.

For the cream filling, whip the cream until light and fluffy, then fold in the raspberries and icing sugar. Spoon the raspberry cream over half the biscuit discs.

For the topping, heat the redcurrant jelly and mix it with the icing sugar until smooth. Spread the icing over the remaining biscuit discs. Sandwich these with the cream-topped discs and decorate with more raspberries. Serve right away.

Rum balls

◇◇

Makes 15

──────

500g/1lb 2oz stale cake, such
  as coffee cakes or Danish
  pastries
200ml/⅞ cup orange juice
2 Tbsp blackcurrant jam
3 Tbsp cocoa powder
1 Tbsp cherry rum, or wine
50g/1¾oz desiccated/shredded
  coconut

Cut the stale cake into small cubes. Place in the bowl of a
food mixer fitted with a dough hook and add all the other
ingredients except the coconut. Mix until you have a thick,
even paste.

Form into 15 round balls each a bit bigger than walnuts.
Roll in a plate of the desiccated coconut and leave to rest in
the refrigerator for 1 hour before eating. (Store them in the
refrigerator, too.)

◇◇◇◇◇◇◇◇◇◇◇◇◇◇◇◇◇◇◇◇

This is a classic Danish leftover cake that all bakers sell. It is made out of all the cakes they did not sell the day before. Everybody knows this, and it is therefore cheap! But it is delicious and a great recipe to have in your repertoire, especially following big celebrations, when cakes might have hung around a little too long afterwards... If you're making these for children, leave out the alcohol!

◇◇◇◇◇◇◇◇◇◇◇◇◇◇◇◇◇◇◇◇

◇◇◇◇◇◇◇◇◇◇◇◇◇◇◇◇◇◇◇◇◇◇◇◇◇

Danish pastries, or *wienerbrød* as we call them, include a range of different small pieces of sweet pastry that we eat in the morning or before lunch. They are never savoury. These ones I used to love as a child, always looking out for them when I went to the bakery in the morning. Very few bakers still make them, but as the home-baked ones also taste so much better, I created my own recipe.

◇◇◇◇◇◇◇◇◇◇◇◇◇◇◇◇◇◇◇◇◇◇◇◇◇

Rose Danish

◇◇

Makes 20–24

For the dough
25g/generous ¾oz fresh yeast
150ml/⅔ cup lukewarm water
1 egg, lightly beaten
1 tsp salt
½ tsp ground cardamom
1 Tbsp caster or granulated
  sugar
325g/2¾ cups 00 grade
  (tipo 00) flour, plus extra
  for dusting
300g/1⅓ cups cold butter,
  thinly sliced
For the glaze and icing
1 egg, beaten
8 Tbsp rose jelly
200g/1¾ cups icing/
  confectioners' sugar

Crumble the yeast into the water, stir to dissolve, then add the egg, salt, cardamom and sugar. Stir in the flour and knead the dough with your hands until it is even and combined. Put it in a bowl, cover with cling film/plastic wrap and leave to rest in the fridge for about 15 minutes.

Roll out the dough on a lightly floured surface into roughly a 45-cm/18-in square. Arrange the butter slices in a square in the centre of the dough, at a 45-degree angle to the corners of the dough so it forms a smaller diamond inside the dough square. Fold the corners of the dough over the butter to encase it fully and seal the joins well.

Roll out the dough again carefully, this time into a rectangle, making sure that it does not crack and expose the butter.

Fold a short end one-third over into the centre, and the other short end over that, as you would a business letter. Wrap in cling film and rest again in the fridge for 15 minutes. Repeat this rolling and folding procedure 3 times in total, remembering to let the dough rest for 15 minutes in the fridge between each.

Roll out the dough on a floured surface to a rectangle about 60 x 40cm/24 x 16in and divide in half. Now roll each out again and fold one half over the other half to make a rectangle, then place on 2 baking sheets lined with baking parchment and let it rise for 30 minutes.

Preheat the oven to 220°C/425°F/gas mark 7. Brush the dough with the beaten egg twice and then bake in the oven for 20 minutes. Leave to cool on a wire rack.

Now make the icing. Melt the rose petal jelly in a pan, add the icing sugar and whisk until smooth. Spread evenly on the pastry and let it settle for 30 minutes. Now cut into 5cm/2in slices.

Coconut macaroons

◇◇

Makes 20

250g/1¼ cups caster or
   granulated sugar
250g/9oz desiccated/shredded
   coconut
4 egg whites
100g/3½oz best dark chocolate,
   at least 60% cocoa solids,
   finely chopped

Preheat the oven to 160°C/325°F/gas mark 3. Mix the sugar and coconut in a bowl. Separately whisk the egg whites until stiff, then mix them well into the coconut mixture. Line a baking sheet with baking parchment and, with a tablespoon, place dollops of the coconut batter on the sheet, making each a bit pointed.

Bake for 8–10 minutes, then leave to cool on a wire rack. Melt the chocolate in a heatproof bowl placed over a saucepan of simmering water; do not let the bowl touch the water. Dip the flat side of each macaroon into it. Leave to set on another piece of baking parchment. These will keep well in an airtight tin for 2 or 3 weeks.

I have been making these since I was a little girl; they are so easy to make. I never bothered to temper the chocolate, mostly because I didn't know you were supposed to, so these are just with melted chocolate. (Of course you can use tempered chocolate if you want a shiny finish, see page 135.)

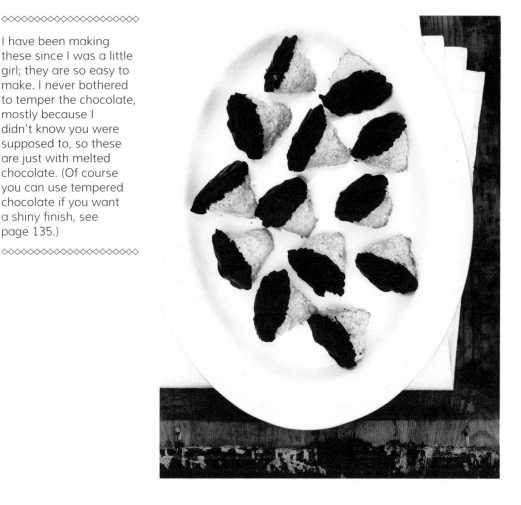

This cake is for people who like things really sweet, such as my husband! Because of the sweetness, it has to be made with homemade raspberry jam that really tastes of the fruit and has a little acidity to it.

Raspberry slices

<><><><><><><><><><><><><><><><><><><><><><><><><><><><><><><><><><><><><><><><><><>

Makes 8

1 quantity Raspberry 'Jam'
  (page 138)
For the base
200g/1½ cups plain/all-purpose
  flour, plus more to dust
50g/5 Tbsp icing/confectioners'
  sugar
100g/scant ½ cup cold butter,
  chopped
½ egg, lightly beaten
For the icing
100g/⅞ cup icing/confectioners'
  sugar
pink sprinkles

To make the base, sift the flour and icing sugar into a bowl and rub in the butter with your fingers until the mixture resembles crumbs. Add the egg and stir until the pastry comes together in a ball. Wrap in cling film/plastic wrap and rest in the refrigerator for 30 minutes.

Preheat the oven to 180°C/350°F/gas mark 4. Roll the dough out on a floured work surface to 40 x 22cm/16 x 9in, then cut this into two 20 x 11cm/8 x 4½in rectangular pieces. Prick each with a skewer all over and bake for 20 minutes. Leave to cool on a wire rack.

Place one of the bases on a sheet of baking parchment. Mix the icing sugar with 2 Tbsp of water and whisk until it has a smooth consistency, then spread evenly on the base. Leave to set for 30 minutes. Place the other base on a wooden chopping board and spread with the raspberry jam. Top with the iced base, sprinkle with the pink sprinkles and cut into smaller triangular pieces. Serve, or keep in an airtight container for 4 or 5 days.

◇◇◇◇◇◇◇◇◇◇◇◇◇◇◇◇◇◇◇◇

This marzipan-filled cake can be dated back to 1856. Denmark had sided with Napoleon in the early 19th century, which cost us dearly: the English bombed Copenhagen and stole our large naval fleet. One of the consequences of that was that Norway won its independence.

◇◇◇◇◇◇◇◇◇◇◇◇◇◇◇◇◇◇◇◇

Napoleon's hat

◇◇◇

Makes 18

For the pastry
200g/1½ cups plain/all-purpose
   flour, plus more to dust
50g/5 Tbsp icing/confectioners'
   sugar
100g/scant ½ cup cold butter,
   chopped
½ egg, lightly beaten
For the filling
100g/½ cup caster or
   granulated sugar
1 egg white, plus ½ egg white
   more, to glaze
250g/8¾oz good marzipan
   (page 136), coarsely grated
For the decoration
150g/5¼oz Tempered Chocolate
   (page 135)

Start by making the pastry. Sift the flour and icing sugar into a bowl. Rub the butter in with your fingers until the mixture resembles crumbs. Add the egg and stir until it comes into a ball. Wrap in cling film/plastic wrap and chill for 30 minutes.

For the filling, beat the sugar with the whole egg white until the sugar dissolves, making sure the mixture does not get too warm. Mix with the marzipan to make a smooth paste. Form it into 18 small balls, each the size of a walnut.

Preheat the oven to 200°C/400°F/gas mark 6. Roll out the pastry on a floured work surface and cut it out with a 6–7cm/2½–2¾in cookie cutter. Take the leftover dough and roll out again, until you have 18 pieces. Place them on a baking sheet lined with baking parchment. Place the marzipan balls in the middle of each. Brush with the egg white to glaze and press the pastry up around the marzipan at 3 equally spaced points, so it looks a bit like Napoleon's famous hat (see the photo, left). Now brush egg white on the other, unglazed side as well. Bake for 10–12 minutes.

Cool on a wire rack and, when cold, dip the flat bases in tempered chocolate – or spread it on with a spatula if you find that easier – and leave to set on a piece of baking parchment, chocolate sides up.

Hot chocolate and sweet buns

〰️

Makes 20 buns

For the buns
50g/2oz fresh yeast
400ml/1⅔ cups lukewarm
  whole milk
100g/scant ½ cup soft butter
1 egg, lightly beaten,
  plus an extra beaten egg
  for brushing
600g/5 cups strong white bread
  flour, plus extra for dusting
1 Tbsp granulated sugar
2 tsp salt
2 tsp ground cardamom
100g/¾ cup raisins
100g/¾ cup dried cranberries
100g/¾ cup hazelnuts, medium
  chopped
For the hot chocolate
350g/¾lb good-quality dark
  chocolate (at least 60% cocoa
  solids), broken into pieces
2 litres/8½ cups whole milk
1–2 Tbsp caster or granulated
  sugar, to taste
200ml/⅞ cup double (heavy)
  cream, whipped, to serve

Crumble the yeast into the milk in a large mixing bowl, stir to dissolve, then mix in the butter and egg. Mix the flour, sugar, salt, cardamom, dried fruits and nuts together, add to the milk mixture and give it a good stir with a wooden spoon to mix. Knead the dough lightly on a floured surface, then replace in the bowl, cover with cling film/plastic wrap and leave to rise for 2 hours.

Knead the dough gently again on a floured surface and form it into 20 buns, then place the buns on baking sheets lined with baking parchment. Cover with tea towels and leave to rise for 30 minutes. Preheat the oven to 200°C/400°F/gas mark 6.

Brush the risen buns with beaten egg and bake in the oven for 20–25 minutes, then leave to cool on a wire rack.

For the hot chocolate, put the chocolate into a heavy-based saucepan and gently melt, stirring all the time, then add a quarter of the milk and stir it into the chocolate, followed by the remaining milk, mixing it well. Now stir in the sugar to taste, then bring the mixture to just under boiling point, stirring constantly so that it doesn't scorch. Take off the heat and pour into mugs. Add spoonfuls of cold whipped cream to the tops and serve with the freshly baked buns, and some butter.

This is a real *hygge* moment: go for a long brisk walk in the woods in the autumn, with the wind in the trees and in your face, then return home to a warm house and enjoy home-baked buns and hot chocolate.

Lingonberry and marzipan cakes

Makes 16

For the cakes
170g/1¼ cups plain/all-purpose flour, plus more to dust
pinch of salt
60g/½ cup icing/confectioners' sugar
115g/½ cup cold butter
½ egg, lightly beaten
For the filling
300g/10½oz good marzipan (page 136), coarsely grated
2 eggs, lightly beaten
100g/scant ½ cup soft butter
150g/5¼oz lingonberries or redcurrants

To make the cakes, sift the flour, salt and icing sugar into a bowl and rub in the butter with your fingers until the mixture resembles crumbs. Add the egg and stir until the pastry comes together in a ball. Wrap in cling film/plastic wrap and rest in the refrigerator for 30 minutes.

Preheat the oven to 200°C/400°F/gas mark 6. Roll the dough out on a floured work surface to 5–8 mm/¼–⅓ in thick, then cut out rounds with a 9cm/3½in cookie cutter. Place them in a fairy cake tin, ideally an ornate one with fluted or oval-shaped holes. Mix the marzipan, eggs and butter into a smooth paste, use it to fill the little pies and add the berries or currants. Bake for 20–25 minutes. Leave to cool on a wire rack before serving.

◇◇

Scandinavians love marzipan. We use it in baking, for decorating cakes, in chocolate bars, and we eat it raw. I like this recipe best with sour lingonberries, because they counterbalance the sweet marzipan.

◇◇

◇◇◇◇◇◇◇◇◇◇◇◇◇◇◇◇◇◇◇

These are small, tasty, luxury cakes. Eating them always makes me feel like I should be in Florence, sitting late at night at Caffè Rivoire at Piazza della Signoria more or less by myself, enjoying the enchanting city.

◇◇◇◇◇◇◇◇◇◇◇◇◇◇◇◇◇◇◇

Florentines

<<<<<<<<<<<<<<<<<<<<<<<<<<<<<<<<<<<<<<<<<<<<<<<<<<<<<<<<<<<<<<<<<<<<<<<<<<<<<<<<<<<<<<<<<

Makes 40 small florentines

150g/¾ cup caster or
  granulated sugar
50g/1¾oz honey
50ml/scant ¼ cup single/light
  cream
50g/3½ Tbsp butter
150g/5¼oz candied orange
  peel, finely chopped
200g/1½ cups blanched
  almonds, sliced
200g/7oz Tempered Chocolate
  (page 135)

In a saucepan, heat the sugar, honey, cream and butter until boiling, then let it boil for a few minutes. Remove from the heat, stir in the candied orange peel and almonds, then cool, cover and place in the refrigerator for 1 hour.

Preheat the oven to 200°C/400°F/gas mark 6.

Place teaspoons of the fruit and nut mixture on baking sheets lined with baking parchment, leaving 3–4cm/1–1½in between each. Bake for 8 minutes, then take them out and push the edges back with a spoon, where they have spread, to make each Florentine smaller once more. Bake for 5–7 minutes longer, until golden brown. Leave to cool a little on the sheets, then carefully transfer to a wire rack with a palette knife to cool completely.

Dip half of each florentine in the chocolate, then place them on a sheet of baking parchment until the chocolate has set.

Smørrebrød
+ Savouries

Salmon and horseradish snitter

◇◇

Serves 8

For the horseradish cream
6 Tbsp full-fat or extra-rich
  Greek yogurt
1 tsp sugar
4 Tbsp grated horseradish
2 Tbsp lemon juice
sea salt and freshly ground
  black pepper
For the snitter
1 cucumber
1 bunch of chervil
2–3 Tbsp lemon juice
6 slices of rye bread
10 slices of smoked salmon

Start with the horseradish cream: mix everything together in a bowl and season to taste. Cover and set aside until needed.

Cut the cucumber into small cubes, chop the chervil and mix it in along with the lemon juice, salt and pepper.

With a 4cm/1½in round cookie cutter, cut out 16 pieces of rye bread and place them on a work surface. Cut the salmon into long slices and roll each into a salmon 'rose'. Place one on each piece of bread and fill with 1 tsp of horseradish cream. Divide the cucumber mix on top of all the *snitter*; the decoration should look a bit rustic, so don't worry if they're not perfect.

Snitter are small pieces of smørrebrød traditionally served at parties in the evening when you wanted to offer a cold meal. Here I top them with smoked salmon, but they can be made with any topping from pages 64–69.

Open sandwiches

◇◇◇

Open sandwiches like this are the most versatile lunch: take the
opportunity to use up leftovers and arrange them on top of a slice
of buttered rye bread for a quick lunch, or pile the toppings high
and make a variety of options for a big gathering.

Left to right: Beef-pickles, Egg-smoked mackerel, Pork-apple salad, Cucumber-goat cheese cream

Beef-pickles

◇◇◇◇◇◇◇◇◇◇◇◇◇◇◇◇◇◇◇◇◇◇◇◇◇◇◇◇◇◇◇

1 slice of rye bread
2 tsp salted butter
80g/2¾oz sliced cooked beef
pickled vegetables
30g/1oz Fried Onions (page 131)
For the horseradish cream
2 Tbsp Greek yogurt
2 tsp freshly grated horseradish
pinch of sugar
1 tsp lemon juice
sea salt and freshly ground black pepper

Mix the ingredients for the horseradish
cream, adding salt and pepper. Butter
the bread, place the beef on top, add
horseradish cream and top with pickled
vegetables and fried onions.

Egg-smoked mackerel

◇◇◇◇◇◇◇◇◇◇◇◇◇◇◇◇◇◇◇◇◇◇◇◇◇◇◇◇◇◇◇

1 slice of rye bread
10g/2 tsp salted butter
1 egg
½ tsp extra virgin olive oil
75g/2½oz smoked mackerel
2 radishes, thinly sliced
1 tsp chopped thyme
sea salt and freshly ground black pepper

Butter the rye bread. Beat the egg with
some salt and pepper and scramble in
a small pan with the olive oil. Place the
scrambled egg on the buttered bread,
divide the mackerel into 2 pieces and place
over the egg. Add the radishes to the top,
decorate with thyme and sprinkle with
pepper to serve.

Pork-apple salad

◇◇

1 slice of rye bread
10g/2 tsp salted butter
100g/3½oz sliced roast pork
1 tsp chopped thyme
leftover crackling (optional)
For the apple salad
2 Tbsp finely diced apple
2 tsp finely chopped mint leaves
1 tsp apple cider vinegar
sea salt and freshly ground black pepper

Butter the rye bread and place the pork
on top. Mix the apple salad ingredients
together, with salt and pepper to taste,
and place on top of the pork. Add the crisp
crackling, if you have some, and the thyme,
sprinkle with salt and pepper and serve.

Cucumber-goat cheese cream

◇◇

50g/1¾oz creamy goat cheese
2 Tbsp baby cress, plus extra to decorate
1 slice of rye bread
3 slices of cucumber
sea salt and freshly ground black pepper

Mix the goat cheese with the baby cress
and season with salt and pepper, then
spread on the rye bread. Place the slices
of cucumber on top and decorate with
extra baby cress.

Egg-tomato

◇◇◇◇◇◇◇◇◇◇◇◇◇◇◇◇◇◇◇◇◇◇◇◇◇◇◇◇◇◇◇◇◇◇◇◇

40g/3 Tbsp butter
4 slices of rye bread
4 tomatoes
4 hard-boiled eggs
4 Tbsp mayonnaise
4 Tbsp cress, or snipped chives
sea salt and freshly ground black pepper

Spread the butter evenly on the bread. Slice the tomatoes and eggs, place next to each other on the rye bread and add 1 Tbsp mayonnaise on top of each slice. Cover the mayonnaise with cress and sprinkle with salt and pepper.

Avocado-prawn

◇◇◇◇◇◇◇◇◇◇◇◇◇◇◇◇◇◇◇◇◇◇◇◇◇◇◇◇◇◇◇◇◇◇◇◇

40g/3 Tbsp butter
4 slices of rye bread
2 avocados
sea salt and freshly ground black pepper
4 Tbsp cottage cheese
200g/7oz prawns/shrimps
a few sprigs of chervil

Spread the butter evenly on the bread. Halve, stone and peel the avocados, slice them into long wedges, then place on the bread and sprinkle with salt and pepper. Spoon 1 Tbsp of cottage cheese on each slice, then arrange the prawns on top with the chervil.

Top to bottom: Avocado-prawn, Egg-tomato

Asparagus tartlets

◇◇

Serves 4

500g/1lb 2oz puff pastry
1 egg, lightly beaten
4–6 crisp Romaine salad
  leaves, to serve
For the filling
300g/10½oz asparagus spears
1 tsp butter
1 small shallot, finely chopped
100ml/⅓ cup dry white wine
200g/7oz shelled peas
100ml/⅓ cup double/heavy
  cream
1 bunch of chervil,
  finely chopped
sea salt and freshly ground
  black pepper

Preheat the oven to 180°C/350°F/gas mark 4. Roll out the puff pastry to 5mm/¼in thick and cut out 8 circles, 9cm/3½in in diameter. Place on a baking sheet lined with baking parchment and brush with the beaten egg. Using a knife tip, score a pattern onto each. Bake for 15–20 minutes, until well risen and golden brown. Take out of the oven and leave on a wire rack to cool.

Meanwhile, make the filling. Cut the asparagus into 2cm/¾in chunks. Heat the butter in a sauté pan, add the shallot and sauté for a few minutes, then add the wine and asparagus and simmer for 5 minutes.

Add the peas and cream, and season. Simmer for 3 minutes, then take off the heat. Cut the puff pastry rounds in half and place the salad inside with the filling.

Tarteletter are rarely homemade, as most people buy them; or if they bake them themselves, they buy the puff pastry dough, which is a great shortcut. Homemade tastes better but sometimes one has to be realistic!

Not a hot dog, but close! A Scandinavian classic for children, served at birthday parties, for TV dinners and at picnics. I add lovage pesto to half of each batch for the adult guests.

Sausage bread rolls

<><><><><><><><><><><><><><><><><><><><><><><><><><><><><><><><><><><><><><><><><><><><><><><><><><>

Makes 20

For the sausage rolls
25g/generous ¾oz fresh yeast
300ml/1¼ cups lukewarm water
450g/3¾ cups strong white
  flour, plus more to dust
2 tsp salt
4 Tbsp finely chopped red onion
20 chipolatas
1 egg, lightly beaten
For the lovage pesto (optional)
1 big bunch of lovage
  (or parsley)
50g/½ cup skin-on almonds
1 garlic clove
1 Tbsp capers, drained
  and rinsed
40g/1½oz hard goat's cheese,
  grated
150ml/⅔ cup olive oil
2–3 Tbsp lemon juice
sea salt and freshly ground
  black pepper

Crumble the yeast into the lukewarm water, stir to dissolve, then stir in the flour and salt and mix well. Knead on a floured work surface to form a smooth dough and add the red onion as you do so. Cover with a tea towel and leave to rise in a warm place for 1 hour.

For the pesto, place all the ingredients except the seasoning in a food processor and blend to a smooth paste, then season to taste with salt and pepper.

Divide the dough into 20 pieces on a lightly floured work surface. Roll each out into a triangle. Place a chipolata in the wide end of a triangle and then roll it up. Repeat to make 10.

Now, for the rolls with pesto, spread the pesto evenly over the remaining 10 dough triangles, place the sausages on the wide ends and roll up as before.

Place the sausage rolls on 2 baking sheets lined with baking parchment, those with the pesto on one sheet and the plain variety on the other. Cover with a tea towel and leave to rise in a warm place for 30 minutes.

Preheat the oven to 200°C/400°F/gas mark 6. Brush each roll with the egg. Bake in the oven for 20–25 minutes until golden brown.

Beetroot is a great vegetable and I try to use it in all kinds of recipes. This savoury muffin is great to eat with a salad at lunch. You can also make the recipe as mini muffins for canapés (these will need less time in the oven). They are a great snack for children and I also bake them to bring along on hikes as an easy lunch. Substitute the bacon for toasted walnuts, if you prefer.

Beetroot and bacon muffins

<><><><><><><><><><><><><><><><><><><><><><><><><><><><><><><><><><><><><><><><>

Makes 10–12

50g/scant ½ cup wholegrain
  stoneground spelt flour
150g/1¼ cups plain/all-purpose
  flour
50g/½ cup jumbo oats
2 tsp baking powder
½ tsp bicarbonate of soda/
  baking soda
1½ tsp salt
1 Tbsp freshly ground black
  pepper
3 eggs
250ml/1 cup full-fat yogurt
4 Tbsp olive oil
200g/7oz raw beetroot,
  finely chopped
100g/3½oz cooked bacon
  lardons, or toasted walnuts
1 Tbsp thyme leaves, plus more
  to serve (optional)

Preheat the oven to 200°C/400°F/gas mark 6.

Mix the flours, oats, baking powder, bicarbonate of soda and salt and pepper in a bowl. In another bowl, beat the eggs with the yogurt and oil. Stir the wet ingredients into the dry, then fold in the beetroot, bacon or nuts and thyme.

Cut out 10–12 x 15cm/6in squares of baking parchment and fold each into a muffin mould. Divide the batter between the prepared moulds and bake in the hot oven for 20–25 minutes.

Serve warm for lunch or dinner, sprinkled with a little more thyme if you like, with a crisp green salad dressed with a mustardy vinaigrette.

Rich cheese crackers

◇◇◇

Makes about 40

600g/4½ cups plain/all-purpose
  flour, plus more to dust
400g/1¾ cups butter, chopped
2 tsp salt
1 egg, beaten
2 Tbsp poppy seeds
2–3 Tbsp sesame seeds
50g/⅔ cup finely grated salty
  cheese, such as cheddar

Tip the flour into a large bowl and rub in the butter with your fingers until the mixture resembles crumbs. Add the salt and splash in just enough water to hold the dough together. Knead on a floured work surface, then return to the mixing bowl, cover and leave to rest in the refrigerator for 1 hour.

Preheat the oven to 200°C/400°F/gas mark 6.

Roll out the dough on a floured work surface into a rectangle, one long side facing you. Fold the left-hand one-third over the centre, then repeat with the right-hand one-third, as though folding a business letter before putting it in an envelope. Turn the package by 90°. Repeat this rolling and folding process twice more, to make a total of 3 times.

Now divide the dough into 3 and roll each out on a floured work surface until 5mm/⅛mm thick. Brush with the egg and sprinkle with poppy seeds, sesame seeds and cheese. Cut into 4cm/1½in squares; a ravioli cutter is good here to give fluted edges. Place on baking sheets lined with baking parchment and bake for 12–15 minutes (you will probably have to bake these in batches). Leave to cool on a wire rack while you bake the rest.

◇◇◇◇◇◇◇◇◇◇◇◇◇◇◇◇◇◇◇◇

This is all about the butter and, as Julia Childs once marvellously said, 'If you're afraid of butter, use cream.' I will add that if you don't like butter, do not bake this cracker! It's the butter that makes it – it's that simple.

◇◇◇◇◇◇◇◇◇◇◇◇◇◇◇◇◇◇◇◇

This recipe is easily doubled if you are cooking for a larger party. You can keep these plain, or sprinkle them with seeds, as you prefer. Any or all of linseeds, poppy or sesame seeds are good.

Rye crispbread

◇◇◇

Makes 40 strips

150ml/⅔ cup lukewarm water
15g/½oz fresh yeast
60g/¾ cup rye flakes
50g/⅔ cup rolled oats
50g/5 Tbsp stoneground rye
    flour, plus more to dust
50g/⅜ cup polenta or cornmeal
75ml/⅓ cup olive oil, plus more
    to brush
1 tsp salt

Pour the water into a bowl and crumble in the yeast, stirring to dissolve. Stir in the rye flakes and oats. Leave to rest for 30 minutes. Now mix in the remaining ingredients. Mix really well, then knead on a floured work surface.

Preheat the oven to 200°C/400°F/gas mark 6.

Divide the dough into four. On a floured work surface, roll each piece out as thinly as possible into a rectangle about 25 x 20cm/10 x 8in. Cut each into 10 strips. Lay the strips on baking sheets lined with baking parchment and brush with oil. Bake for 10–12 minutes (you will probably have to bake these in batches).

Leave to cool on a wire rack while you bake the rest.

'Shower buns'

<><><><><><><><><><><><><><><><><><><><><><><><><><><><><><><><><><><><><><><><><><><><><><><>

Makes 20

15g/½oz fresh yeast
700ml/3 cups cold water
8g/1½ tsp salt
850–900g/7–7½ cups strong
  white flour

Crumble the yeast into the water, stir to dissolve, then add the salt and flour and mix well. The dough is sticky, so don't use your hands for kneading; use a food processor fitted with a dough hook or a wooden spoon. Cover the bowl with cling film/plastic wrap and refrigerate overnight.

The next day, preheat the oven to 240°C/475°F/gas mark 9, or as hot as it will go.

Gently cut away enough dough for the number of buns you wish to bake and shape them into rolls, handling them as little as possible. Place on a baking sheet lined with baking parchment and slash each bun with a cross, using a razor blade or a very sharp knife.

Bake for 5 minutes, then reduce the oven temperature to 210°C/410°F/gas mark 6½ and bake for 15–20 minutes, while you take a shower. Get them out of the oven and leave to rest for 5 minutes before eating for breakfast.

Keep the dough in the refrigerator and bake some rolls every morning. It will keep in the refrigerator for up to 5 days.

◇◇◇

Make this dough in 10 minutes and then you can use it in the mornings
for fresh-made rolls. They bake in the time that you shower! You can play
around with the dough and swap some of the wheat flour for other types.

◇◇◇

These are very good served as simple but super-healthy open sandwiches with cheese or salmon on the day they are baked, but also great toasted the next morning and eaten with cheddar or marmalade: a Scandi-Anglo crossover. Rye does contain gluten but, nevertheless, this bread is easy on the digestion for those who have a wheat intolerance.

Mini Finnish rye breads

◇◇◇

Makes 20

Day 1
15g/½oz fresh yeast
200ml/⅞ cup lukewarm water
200ml/⅞ cup cold buttermilk
100g/¾ cup stoneground
  rye flour

Day 2
400ml/1⅔ cups lukewarm water
10g/⅓oz fresh yeast
600g/5 cups stoneground rye
  flour, plus more to dust
2 tsp salt

Day 1
Crumble the yeast into the lukewarm water in a large bowl, then mix in the buttermilk and rye flour. Cover with cling film/plastic wrap and leave overnight at room temperature.

Day 2
Pour the lukewarm water into another large bowl, then crumble in the yeast and add the buttermilk mixture from Day 1. Mix well, then add the flour and salt. Now start kneading with your hands in the bowl. It is very sticky, the idea is just to work the flour into the dough. Cover with cling film and leave for 4 hours at room temperature.

Now flour your hands very well with rye flour and make 20 small flat breads, each about 8cm/3in in diameter, from the dough. Place them on baking sheets lined with baking parchment, cover with tea towels and leave to rise in a warm place for 30 minutes. Preheat the oven to 200°C/400°F/gas mark 6. Now prick lots of holes in the breads with a skewer, brush with water and bake for 30 minutes. Leave to cool on a wire rack.

Easy morning spelt rolls

◇◇

Makes 14

10g/⅓oz fresh yeast
700ml/3 cups cold water
400g/2¾ cups fine spelt flour,
  plus extra for dusting
350g/2⅞ cups wholegrain
  spelt flour
50g/1¾oz spelt flakes
1 tsp salt

Day 1
Dissolve the yeast in the water in a bowl, add both flours, the spelt flakes and the salt, mix well for about 10 minutes, then cover and refrigerate overnight.

Day 2
Preheat the oven to 230°C/450°F/gas mark 8.

Place the dough on a floured work surface and knead lightly. Form into 14 rolls and place on a baking sheet lined with baking parchment. Spray some cold water in the oven to create steam, then bake the rolls for 10 minutes. Now turn down the oven temperature to 200°C/400°F/gas mark 6 and bake for another 10–15 minutes. Leave to cool on a wire rack before eating.

These rolls are really easy to make, and the dough more or less takes care of itself. I serve these spelt rolls in the morning, or with soup at night.

◇◇◇◇◇◇◇◇◇◇◇◇◇◇◇◇◇◇◇◇◇◇◇

These are weird little dry things, kind of a savoury biscotti that we like to make and keep in tins, then eat for breakfast, lunch and snacks. I like them best with salmon and cream cheese – an all-time Scandinavian classic.

◇◇◇◇◇◇◇◇◇◇◇◇◇◇◇◇◇◇◇◇◇◇◇

Rye crackers

◇◇

Makes 24

Day 1
25g/generous ¾oz fresh yeast
300ml/1¼ cups buttermilk
100g/¾ cup wholegrain
  stoneground rye flour
Day 2
25g/generous ¾oz fresh yeast
200ml/⅞ cup water
50ml/scant ¼ cup golden/corn
  syrup
150g/⅔ cup cold butter
200g/1⅔ cups wholegrain
  stoneground rye flour
300g/2½ cups strong white
  bread flour
2 tsp salt
100g/3½oz rye flakes
1 tsp each of fennel seeds,
  anise seeds and caraway
  seeds, lightly crushed

Day 1
Mix the yeast, buttermilk and rye flour together in a small bowl, cover with a tea towel and leave overnight at room temperature.

Day 2
Add the yeast and water to the overnight starter mixture with the syrup. Cut the butter into cubes. Mix the flours in a bowl and crumble in the butter, mixing with your fingers until it resembles breadcrumbs. Add the salt, rye flakes and crushed seeds, then add the starter mixture and mix to a firm dough. Cover and leave to rise for 1 hour, then form the dough into 24 small oval rolls and place them on baking sheets lined with baking parchment. Cover with tea towels and leave to rise for 40 minutes.

Preheat the oven to 200°C/400°F/gas mark 6. Bake for 15 minutes, then transfer to a wire rack to cool and reduce the oven temperature to 150°C/300°F/gas mark 2. When cool, split each skorper in half with a knife, and place the halves back on the baking sheets. Bake in the oven for 25 minutes, then leave to cool before eating. Stored in an airtight container, they will keep for weeks.

Classic bread rolls

<<<<<<<<<<<<<<<<<<<<<<<<<<<<<<<<<<<<<<<<<<<<<<<<<<<<<<<<<<<<<<<<<<<<<<

Makes 20

Day 1
20g/¾oz fresh yeast
300ml/1¼ cups lukewarm water
150g/1¼ cups stoneground
  rye flour

Day 2
75g/⅓ cup butter, melted and
  left to cool a little
300ml/1¼ cups lukewarm water
10g/⅓oz fresh yeast
700g/5¾ cups strong white
  flour, plus more to dust
2 tsp salt
1 egg, lightly beaten
poppy seeds, to top

Day 1
Crumble the yeast into the lukewarm water in a large bowl and stir to dissolve. Add the flour, mix it in well, then cover with a tea towel and leave overnight at room temperature.

Day 2
Mix the butter well into yesterday's dough with the water, then crumble in the yeast. Separately mix the flour and salt, then mix it into the yeast mixture and stir until you have a smooth dough. Cover with a tea towel and leave to rise for 2 hours at room temperature.

On a well-floured work surface, form 20 very round and perfect rolls. Place on baking sheets lined with baking parchment, cover with tea towels and leave to rise again, in a warm place, for 30 minutes.

Preheat the oven to 220°C/425°F/gas mark 7.

Brush the rolls with the egg, leave for 3 minutes, then brush them all again. Dredge them with poppy seeds. Spray cold water in the oven to create steam and bake for 10 minutes, then reduce the oven temperature to 200°C/400°F/gas mark 6 and bake for another 15 minutes. Leave to cool on a wire rack.

These are classic rolls, perfect with just butter and cheese.

◇◇◇

In the more than 20 years in which I have been coming to the UK,
openness to rye has never been greater. Many of my friends now bake
rye bread and mixed-grain breads containing rye flour.

◇◇◇

Rye rolls

<<<<<<<<<<<<<<<<<<<<<<<<<<<<<<<<<<<<<<<<<<<<<<<<<<<<<<<<<<<<<<<<<<<<<<<<<<<

Makes 20

50g/2oz fresh yeast
700ml/3 cups lukewarm water
2 Tbsp barley malt syrup
400g/3⅓ cups stoneground
  rye flour
500g/4¼ cups strong white
  flour, plus more to dust
1 tsp salt
cold coffee and rye flakes,
  to glaze and top

Crumble the yeast into the lukewarm water, stir to dissolve, then add the syrup. Mix the 2 flours and the salt into the yeast mixture and stir until the dough is smooth. Knead on a floured work surface, then return to the bowl, cover with a tea towel and leave to rise at room temperature for 2 hours.

Now form into 20 small oval rolls and place on baking sheets lined with baking parchment. Cover again with a tea towel and leave to rise again, in a warm place, for 30 minutes. Preheat the oven to 200°C/400°F/gas mark 6.

Slash the rolls on top with a razor blade or sharp knife, then brush with cold coffee and sprinkle with rye flakes. Spray cold water in the oven to create steam and bake for 30 minutes. Leave to cool on a wire rack.

Celebrations

Raspberry éclairs

◇◇

Makes 8–10

For the choux pastry
1 quantity Choux pastry dough
  (page 136)
butter, for the baking parchment
For the cream filling
200ml/⅞ cup double/heavy
  cream
2 Tbsp icing/confectioners'
  sugar
1 vanilla pod/bean
200g/7oz raspberries
For the icing
150g/5¼oz best dark chocolate,
  at least 60% cocoa solids
15g/1 Tbsp butter

Preheat the oven to 200°C/400°F/gas mark 6.

Put the dough in a piping bag fitted with a 1cm/⅜in plain nozzle. Pipe a 10cm/4in line of choux pastry on a baking sheet lined with buttered baking parchment. Follow with a second line parallel to the first, so that they cling together. Pipe a third line on top of the other two. Move away from this first bun, giving it plenty of space on the tray, then repeat. You need to pipe 8–10 of these.

Bake for 20–30 minutes; do not open the oven door for the first 10 minutes or the pastry may not rise. The pastries are done when they are golden brown and firm. Transfer to a wire rack and, with a sharp knife, pierce holes in the side of each bun, to let the steam out. Leave to cool.

Whip the cream until billowing and fold in the icing sugar. Slit the vanilla pod lengthways with a sharp knife and scrape out the seeds with the tip. Add to the cream with the raspberries, whipping again briefly to mix in the vanilla and roughly break up the berries. Split each choux bun in half horizontally and place a couple of spoonfuls of cream on the bottom half. Place the other half on top, being careful not to press them together.

Break the chocolate into pieces, place in a small heatproof bowl and fit over a saucepan of simmering water; the bowl should not touch the water. When it has melted, remove from the heat and stir in the butter. Spread the chocolate mixture on top of the éclairs and leave to set before serving.

I really like choux pastry as a base for cakes because it is not sweet, and I love the texture. Here is my summer éclair: easy to make, and containing fresh berries.

Walnut kisses

◇◇◇

Makes 40

4 egg whites
250g/1¼ cups caster/superfine
  sugar
½ tsp vinegar
150g/5¼oz walnuts, chopped

Preheat the oven (not fan) to 110°C/225°F/gas mark ¼.
Line 2 baking sheets with baking parchment.

Using an electric hand whisk, whisk the egg whites until
stiff, then whisk in the sugar 1 tbsp at a time, until very stiff
and all the sugar has been added. Add the vinegar and fold
in the chopped walnuts.

Using 2 spoons, place dollops of the meringue mixture
on the sheets (not too neat; they should look rustic). Bake
for 1 hour, then turn off the heat, open the oven door and
leave it ajar for 15 minutes. Take the meringues out of the
oven and leave to cool completely on a wire rack, still on
their sheets of baking parchment.

Serve right away, or pack into cellophane bags and give
away as gifts. They last for weeks in a cake tin. They are
also great crushed over ice cream.

In Danish we call a small meringue a kiss, or kys, because they are as delightful as one. Sweet, crunchy and melting like air in the mouth.

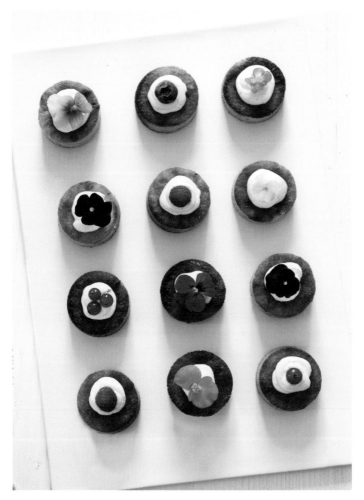

When I was a child, my siblings, cousins and I loved our grandmother's mazarin cake. It was a crazy green from the food colouring and probably tasted more artificial than I would appreciate today. I once discussed with one of my cousins whether we should try making it again, and we agreed just to let that cake remain a happy memory. Here is the recipe for the mazarin cakes I bake today.

Mazarin cakes

◇◇

Makes 24

250g/8¾oz good marzipan
(page 136), grated
250g/1¼ cups caster/superfine
sugar
250g/1 generous cup soft butter,
plus extra for greasing
5 eggs
70g/½ cup plain/all-purpose
flour
blueberries, raspberries,
redcurrants and edible flowers,
to decorate
For the frosting
1 vanilla pod/bean
200ml/⅞ cup full-fat crème
fraîche
2 Tbsp icing/confectioners'
sugar

Preheat the oven to 190°C/375°F/gas mark 5.

Beat the grated marzipan with the sugar in a mixing bowl (you get the best result using an electric mixer), then add the butter and beat again until smooth. Add the eggs one at a time, beating between additions, until the mixture is even and smooth, then fold in the flour. Transfer the mixture to a piping bag and pipe into silicone mini-muffin moulds, about 3cm/1¼in in diameter (just use a spoon if you don't have a piping bag), filling the moulds to just below the rim. Now bake in the oven for 10 minutes then remove and leave to cool in the silicone moulds.

For the frosting, split the vanilla pod in half lengthways and scrape out the seeds using the tip of a knife. Put the crème fraîche in a mixing bowl, add the vanilla seeds and whisk until stiff, using an electric mixer or stand mixer. Stir in the icing sugar and transfer to a clean piping bag (if you have one, or you can use a spoon) and refrigerate until ready to use.

When the mazarins have cooled, take them out of the moulds, pipe a small dollop of frosting onto each, then decorate with the berries and edible flowers.

Marzipan cream buns

◇◇

Makes 20

For the buns
50g/2oz fresh yeast
400ml/1⅔ cups lukewarm
  whole milk
200g/⅞ cup crème fraîche
100g/scant ½ cup butter, melted
1–1.1kg/8⅓–9 cups 00 grade
  (tipo 00) flour, plus more
  to dust
1 tsp salt
100g/½ cup caster or
  granulated sugar
1 egg, lightly beaten
icing/confectioners' sugar,
  to dust
For the filling
150g/5¼oz good marzipan
  (page 136), coarsely grated
6 Tbsp double/heavy cream
200ml/⅞ cup whipping cream

Dissolve the yeast in the milk, then add the crème fraîche, butter and 100ml/7 Tbsp water. Mix 1kg/8⅓ cups of the flour with the salt and sugar, then mix this into the yeast mixture. Knead on a floured work surface with the remaining flour if needed to form a smooth, firm dough. Leave to rise in a warm place for 2 hours. Form into 20 very round buns, then leave to rise, again in a warm place, for 30 minutes.

Preheat the oven to 200°C/400°F/gas mark 6. Brush the buns with the egg and bake for 25 minutes. Place on a wire rack to cool. When cold, cut the tops off, set them aside, and take out some of the crumb from the inside to form little hollows for the filling.

Put the breadcrumbs from about 5 of the buns into a bowl, then add the marzipan and double cream. Mix well. With a teaspoon, place the filling inside the semlor. Whip the whipping cream and place in a piping bag fitted with a 1cm/⅜in nozzle. Pipe the cream on top of the marzipan filling and to the edges of the buns. Replace the tops of the buns, sift over some icing sugar and serve right away.

This was originally the last festive food cooked and served before Lent, the fasting period in northern Europe. Today, *semlor* are eaten in Sweden from shortly after Christmas until Easter.

These mini scones became part of my 'cake table' when I lived in London in the early 1990s. There I learned about afternoon tea when my Danish granny (*mormor*) experienced afternoon tea at the Ritz. She chose coffee rather than tea, and her favourite cakes among the afternoon tea selection were the scones, with clotted cream and jam.

Buttermilk scones with cream and jam

<><><><><><><><><><><><><><><><><><><><><><><><><><><><><><><><><><><><>

Makes 14–16

400g/3 cups plain/all-purpose flour, plus more to dust
5 Tbsp caster or granulated sugar
2 tsp salt
3 tsp baking powder
150g/⅔ cup cold butter, chopped
200ml/⅞ cup buttermilk
300ml/1¼ cups double/heavy cream, to serve
Gooseberry and Vanilla 'Jam' or Raspberry 'Jam', to serve (page 138)

Preheat the oven to 180°C/350°F/gas mark 4.

Sift the flour, sugar, salt and baking powder into a big bowl, add the cold butter and, with your fingers, rub the butter into the flour until it has the consistency of crumbs. Add the buttermilk and fold in until the dough becomes smooth. Remove from the bowl and knead on a floured work surface until the texture is even, but do not overwork, then roll the dough out to 2cm/¾in thick. Fold the dough in half, then roll it out to 2cm/¾in thick again. Repeat this folding and rolling three times, then finish by rolling the dough out to 1.5cm/½in thick.

With a 4cm/1½in round cookie cutter, cut out 14–16 scones and place on a baking sheet lined with baking parchment. Bake in the oven for 15–18 minutes. Leave on a wire rack until just cold.

Whip the cream until billowing and serve with the scones and the jam. I put the cream on first, then the jam, but this is a contentious issue, so just do as you prefer! Serve right away, and definitely on the same day they are baked.

Choux pastries with rhubarb cream

◇◇◇

Makes 16–18

For the pastries
1 quantity Choux pastry dough
  (page 136)
butter, for the baking parchment
For the rhubarb cream
1 vanilla pod/bean
300g/10½oz rhubarb
150g/¾ cup caster/superfine
  sugar
200ml/⅞ cup whipping cream
icing/confectioners' sugar,
  to dust

Preheat the oven to 200°C/400°F/gas mark 6. Line a baking sheet with baking parchment and butter it lightly.

With 2 teaspoons, place walnut-sized pieces of the dough on the baking sheet a few centimetres apart; you should get 16–18. Bake for 20–25 minutes; do not open the oven door for the first 10 minutes or the pastry may not rise. The pastries are done when they are golden brown and firm. Transfer to a wire rack and, with a sharp knife, pierce holes in the side of each bun, to let the steam out. Leave to cool.

Meanwhile, reduce the oven temperature to 180°C/350°F/gas mark 4. Cut the vanilla pod in half lengthways and scrape out the seeds with a sharp knife. Cut the rhubarb into 1cm/⅜in thick slices, place in a baking dish and mix in the sugar and vanilla seeds. Bake for about 15 minutes, then leave to cool completely.

Whip the cream until it is quite stiff, then fold into the rhubarb. Cut each choux pastry in half and place 2–3 Tbsp of the rhubarb cream in the middle. Dust with icing sugar and serve right away.

Choux pastry can be a challenge to work with the first couple of times you make it, but you will master it eventually. When I first started my catering company, these were often on the menu for parties. Everybody loves them!

Holiday crunchy cardamom buns

<><><><><><><><><><><><><><><><><><><><><><><><><><><><><><><><><><><><><>

Makes 20 buns (40 halves)

50g/2oz fresh yeast
250ml/1 cup lukewarm
  whole milk
110g/½ cup butter, melted
  and left to cool a little
1 egg, lightly beaten, plus
  more to glaze
2 Tbsp caster or granulated
  sugar
450g/3¾ cups 00 grade (tipo
  00) flour, plus more to dust
1 tsp salt
1 tsp ground cardamom

Crumble the yeast into the milk, stir to dissolve, then mix
in the butter well and add the egg. In a separate bowl,
mix the sugar, flour, salt and cardamom together, then stir
it into the yeast mixture and mix well. Knead on a floured
work surface until you have a smooth dough. Place in a
large bowl, cover with a tea towel and leave to rise for
2 hours at room temperature.

Form 20 very square buns, making them as perfect as
possible. Place 1cm/⅜in apart on a baking sheet lined with
baking parchment. Cover with tea towels and leave to rise
at room temperature for 30 minutes.

Preheat the oven to 220°C/425°F/gas mark 7.

Brush the rolls with egg and bake in the oven for
20 minutes. Leave to cool on a wire rack.

When the rolls are cold, preheat the oven again to
200°C/400°F/gas mark 6. Cut each roll in half, place them
cut sides up on baking sheets lined with baking parchment
and toast them in the oven for seven to 10 minutes. Serve
right away with butter.

Hveder are served on Denmark's big prayer day in May, which should be dedicated to praying. Today the tradition is that we buy or bake *hveder* on the day before the prayer day and eat them warm at night with butter.

Pink meringue kisses

◇◇◇

Makes 35–40

---

4 large egg whites
250g/1¼ cups caster/superfine
  sugar
1 Tbsp white wine vinegar
1 tsp pink food colouring, or
  1 tsp juice from raw beetroot

Preheat the oven to 110°C/225°F/gas mark ¼.

Line 2 baking sheets with baking parchment. Whisk the egg whites until stiff, but do not beat them too much. Gradually whisk in the sugar a spoon at a time, then add the vinegar and food colouring or beetroot juice.

Using 2 tablespoons, place big dollops of the pink meringue on the baking sheets, each a few centimetres apart. Bake for 45–50 minutes, then cool on the baking parchment on a wire rack.

Crunchy on the outside, soft inside and sweeter than sweet: these are just so irresistible. We call them kys, which means kiss in Danish. If you prefer to stay away from artificial food colouring you can use raw beetroot juice.

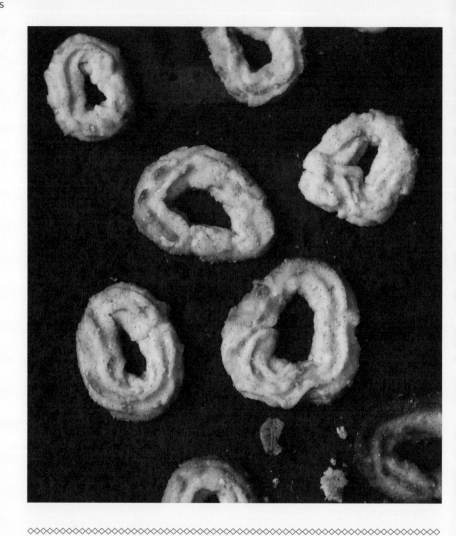

It would not be Christmas without these. I use a star-shaped extruder fitted to the mincer attachment of my food mixer to give them a ridged surface. However, it's easy to roll them by hand, too.

Vanilla cookies

◇◇◇

Makes 70

2 vanilla pods/beans
175g/1⅓ cups plain/all-purpose
  flour, plus more to dust
125g/⅔ cup caster or
  granulated sugar
pinch of salt
200g/⅞ cup butter, chopped
100g/1 cup ground almonds
1 egg yolk

Split the vanilla pods lengthways and scrape out the seeds with a sharp knife. Sift the flour, sugar and salt into a bowl, then rub in the butter with your fingers until the mixture resembles crumbs. Add the ground almonds and vanilla seeds. Now add the egg yolk, working the mixture with your fingers until the dough forms a ball. Knead on a lightly floured work surface for 1–2 minutes, then wrap in cling film/plastic wrap and chill overnight.

When ready to bake, preheat the oven to 200°C/400°F/ gas mark 6. Roll the dough into 70 sausages, each 5–6 x 1cm/2 x ⅜in long. Curl each into a ring and press the ends together. Or use a food processor and star-shaped dough extruder (see recipe introduction). Place on baking sheets lined with baking parchment and bake for about 7 minutes. (You will probably need to bake these in batches.) Cool on a wire rack, then store in an airtight container for 3–4 weeks, though there's no way they will last that long.

Rye and orange cookies

<><><><><><><><><><><><><><><><><><><><><><><><><><><><><><><><><><><><><><>

Makes about 35

50g/3½ Tbsp butter
125g/1½ cups rye flakes
250g/1¼ cups caster or
   granulated sugar
2 eggs, lightly beaten
2 Tbsp plain/all-purpose flour,
   sifted
2 tsp baking powder
2 tsp finely grated organic
   orange zest
pinch of salt

Preheat the oven to 180°C/350°F/gas mark 4. Melt the butter and mix it with the rye flakes in a bowl. Stir in the sugar and eggs. In another bowl, mix the flour, baking powder, orange zest and salt. Stir this into the rye mixture.

Use 2 teaspoons to drop small mounds of the mixture on to a baking sheet lined with baking parchment, spacing them out well.

Bake in the oven for about 10 minutes, then leave to cool a little before using a palette knife to transfer them to a wire rack. (You may have to bake these in batches.) When cold, store in an airtight tin for up to 3 weeks.

This super-easy dough needs no resting or kneading, so even novice bakers will make these successfully on their first attempt. I always bake them for Christmas.

This was my grandfather's favourite cookie. He loved Christmas, just as I do now. He made sure that all the traditions were kept, but it was his presence and love for his family that made Christmas so magical for us.

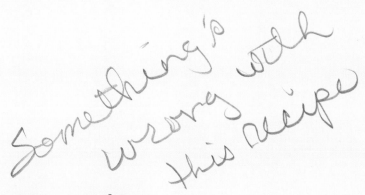

Finnish sugar cookies

◇◇◇

Makes 35

250g/2 cups plain/all-purpose
   flour
75g/6 Tbsp granulated sugar,
   plus more for the top
200g/⅞ cup butter, chopped
2 Tbsp finely grated organic
   lemon zest
1 egg, lightly beaten

Sift the flour into a bowl and mix in the sugar, butter and lemon zest, first by rubbing with your fingers and then by mixing with a wooden spoon, until the dough is smooth and firm. Wrap in cling film/plastic wrap and place in the refrigerator for 1 hour.

Preheat the oven to 190°C/375°F/gas mark 5.

Now place the dough between 2 sheets of baking parchment and roll it out to a rectangle about 1.5cm/½in thick. Remove the top layer of baking parchment.

Brush the dough with egg and dredge sugar densely on top. Carefully roll over it with a rolling pin, so the sugar is pressed slightly into the dough to make the crisp topping to these cookies. Cut into 3 x 2cm/1 x ¾in pieces, place them on baking sheets lined with fresh baking parchment and bake for 15–18 minutes. Leave to cool on a wire rack.

When they are completely cold, store them in an airtight container. They should keep for 2–3 weeks.

Almond cookies

<><><><><><><><><><><><><><><><><><><><><><><><><><><><><><><><><><><><><><><><><><><><><><><><>

Makes 40

200g/1 cup caster or granulated
  sugar
200g/1½ cups plain/all-purpose
  flour, sifted, plus more to dust
75g/¾ cup ground almonds
200g/⅞ cup cold butter,
  chopped
1 egg, lightly beaten

Mix the sugar, flour and almonds in a bowl. Rub in the butter with your fingers until the mixture resembles crumbs. Work in the egg, again with your fingers, until you get an even dough, then wrap in cling film/plastic wrap and leave to rest in the refrigerator for one hour.

When ready to bake, preheat the oven to 200°C/400°F/gas mark 6. Roll out the dough on a lightly floured work surface and cut out shapes with a cookie cutter. At this stage you can make a little hole in the top of each, so they can be hung up later. Place them on a baking sheet lined with baking parchment.

Bake for 5 minutes, then leave to cool on a wire rack, re-piercing the holes for hanging if necessary while the cookies are still warm (they may have closed up as they were baking).

This dough is good for when you are baking with children, as the cookies can be cut into all kinds of shapes. Here, I have made angels, trees and stars.

Baking with honey and spices goes back centuries in Scandinavia. These are full of flavour and become even better as the days go by; they can last for 2–3 weeks! Black tea and honey bombs, served toasted with butter, are a match made in heaven.

Honey bombs

<><><><><><><><><><><><><><><><><><><><><><><><><><><><><><><><><><><><><><><><><><><><><><><><><><>

Makes 16–18

150g/5¼oz honey
150g/¾ cup soft brown sugar
150g/⅔ cup butter
4 eggs
400g/3 cups plain/all-purpose
  flour
2 tsp bicarbonate of soda/
  baking soda
4 tsp ground cinnamon
3 tsp ground cloves
200g/7oz candied mixed peel

Preheat the oven to 180°C/350°F/gas mark 4.

Gently melt the honey, sugar and butter in a saucepan. Leave the mixture to cool a little, then beat in the eggs one by one. In a separate large bowl, sift the flour, bicarbonate of soda and spices, then stir this into the honey mixture and add the mixed peel.

Divide the batter between mini tart tins, each 8–9cm/3–3½in in diameter, so that it lies about 1cm/⅜in deep (you will probably have to cook these in batches). Bake for 20–25 minutes, then leave to cool on a wire rack while you cook the rest.

Christmas stars

<<<<<<<<<<<<<<<<<<<<<<<<<<<<<<<<<<<<<<<<<<<<<<<<<<<<<<<<<<<<<<<<<<<<<<<<<<<<<<<<<<<<<<<<<<<<<<<<<<<<<<<<<<<<<<

Makes 24

200g/7oz prunes, pitted
50g/¼ cup caster or granulated
  sugar
4 Tbsp lemon juice
1 quantity Basic Danish pastry
  dough (page 132)
plain/all-purpose flour, to dust
1 egg, lightly beaten

Chop the prunes and put them in a saucepan. Pour in 100ml/7 Tbsp water, then add the sugar and lemon juice. Place over a medium heat and bring to the boil, then reduce the heat and simmer for 5 minutes. Stir every now and then, until you have a smooth-ish compote. Leave to cool.

Roll out the pastry dough on a floured work surface to a 60 x 40cm/24 x 16in rectangle. Cut it into 10cm/4in squares.

Place 1–2 tsp of prune filling in the middle of each dough square. Slit each corner, towards the middle, with a 3cm/1in long cut. Fold alternate tips of the slit corners towards the centre, pressing them together firmly so they create a star shape (see photo, right). Place on baking sheets lined with baking parchment, cover with tea towels and leave to rise at room temperature for 30 minutes.

Preheat the oven to 220°C/425°F/gas mark 7.

Brush the pastries all over with the egg. Bake for 5 minutes, then reduce the oven temperature to 200°C/400°F/gas mark 6 and bake for 10–15 minutes more, or until golden brown. Leave to cool on a wire rack.

◇◇◇◇◇◇◇◇◇◇◇◇◇◇◇◇◇◇◇◇◇◇

These are traditional in
Finland. In Scandinavia,
we have always used
prunes at Christmas. In
the old days you could
not find fresh fruit in the
winter, only dried and
preserved.

◇◇◇◇◇◇◇◇◇◇◇◇◇◇◇◇◇◇◇◇◇◇

There is a pastry for all seasons, such as the ones with jam I make in the summer. When it's cold outside and my world is covered in snow and silence, I like something spicy which goes well with a hot drink. This is excellent with a glass of White gløgg (see page 129). I serve these pastries with gløgg every year at my Christmas staff party.

Winter spiced pastry

<><><><><><><><><><><><><><><><><><><><><><><><><><><><><><><><><><><><><><><><><><><><>

Makes 20

25g/generous ¾oz fresh yeast
150ml/⅔ cup lukewarm water
1 egg, lightly beaten, plus
    1 more to brush
2 Tbsp caster or granulated
    sugar
½ tsp salt
325g/2¾ cups 00 grade (tipo
    00) flour, sifted, plus more
    to dust
2 tsp ground cinnamon
1 tsp ground coriander
1 tsp ground cardamom
50g/½ cup raisins
50g/1¾oz mixed candied peel
250g/1 generous cup cold
    butter, sliced

In a mixing bowl, crumble the yeast into the water and stir to dissolve. Stir in the egg, sugar and salt. In a separate large bowl, combine the flour, spices, raisins and candied peel, then stir in the yeast mixture until the dough comes together and leaves the edge of the bowl. Turn it on to a floured work surface and knead for 5 minutes until shiny but not sticky. Return it to the bowl, cover with cling film/plastic wrap and refrigerate for 15 minutes.

Now roll out the dough on a lightly floured work surface into a 50cm/20in square. Spread the sliced butter over the dough, about 10cm/4in in from the edge, so the square of dough has a smaller square of butter on top. Fold the corners of the dough over the butter so they meet in the centre, making a smaller square parcel.

Carefully roll the dough into a 60 x 40cm/24 x 16in rectangle, making sure it doesn't crack and that the butter stays inside the parcel.

Next you want to fold the dough so that the butter is layered within it. Starting from a short side, fold the bottom third of dough over the middle third, then fold the top third down over that, as if folding a business letter. Roll it out again, then fold into 3 in the same way. Repeat 3 times, wrapping the dough in cling film and resting it in the refrigerator between each repeat for 15 minutes. Finally, roll out the dough on a floured work surface and cut out 20 squares. Take each one and press all the corners together. Place, corners down, on a baking sheet lined with baking parchment. Cover with tea towels and leave to rise for one hour in a warm place.

Preheat the oven to 220°C/425°F/gas mark 7. Brush the pastries with the egg and bake them for 10 minutes, then reduce the oven temperature to 200°C/400°F/gas mark 6 and bake for 10–15 minutes more, keeping an eye on them so they do not turn too dark. Leave to cool on a wire rack.

The classic Scandinavian marzipan cake. When I was growing up it was only served at parties, weddings or for New Year's Eve. I love *kransekage*, so for me New Year's Eve was something special to look forward to.

Marzipan cakes

<><><><><><><><><><><><><><><><><><><><><><><><><><><><><><><><><><><><>

Makes 24

100g/¾ cup blanched almonds
200g/1 cup caster/superfine
  sugar
3 egg whites
500g/1lb 2oz good marzipan
  (page 136)
200g/7oz Tempered Chocolate
  (page 135)

Whizz the almonds and sugar together in a food processor until finely ground. Add the egg whites and whizz again until you have a smooth, white mixture. Work quickly to make sure it does not get too hot in the processor; otherwise the egg whites start clotting. Grate the marzipan and blend it into the almond mixture. Transfer to a bowl, cover tightly and rest in the refrigerator for a couple of hours, or even overnight.

When you're ready to bake, preheat the oven to 190°C/375°F/gas mark 5.

Shape the mixture into 24 rectangular cakes, each about 2cm/¾in wide and 5cm/2in long, like shortbread fingers. Place on a baking sheet lined with baking parchment and bake for 15–18 minutes. Leave to cool on a wire rack.

With a spoon or a whisk, decorate with the tempered chocolate, just lightly drizzling the chocolate back and forth.

Little spiced apple pies

<<<<<<<<<<<<<<<<<<<<<<<<<<<<<<<<<<<<<<<<<<<<<<<<<<<<<<<<<<<<<<<<<<<<<<<<

Makes 20 pies

For the pastry
110g/¾ cup icing/confectioners'
sugar, plus more to dust
(optional)
340g/2½ cups plain/all-purpose
flour, plus more to dust
pinch of salt
225g/1 cup cold butter, chopped
1 egg, lightly beaten, plus
more to glaze
For the filling
400g/14oz tart eating apples
100g/½ cup caster or
granulated sugar
1 tsp ground cinnamon
¼ tsp ground cloves
½ tsp ground cardamom
½ tsp freshly ground
black pepper
50ml/3½ Tbsp calvados

For the pastry, sift the icing sugar, flour and salt together, then mix in the butter, either in a food processor or by rubbing it in with your fingers, until it has the consistency of crumbs. Add the egg and mix the dough until it is firm and smooth. Wrap in cling film/plastic wrap and let it rest in the refrigerator for at least 1 hour, or overnight.

Peel the apples, core them and cut into small cubes, then tip into a saucepan with the sugar and spices and simmer for 10 minutes. Add the calvados and let it simmer for 5 minutes more, then leave to cool.

When the apple mixture is cold and you are ready to bake, preheat the oven to 180°C/350°F/gas mark 4.

Roll the dough out on a floured work surface to 5–8 mm/⅛–⅓mm thick, cut out 20 rounds with a 7cm/2¾in cookie cutter and place them in 2 non-stick fairy cake tins. Fill with the apple sauce.

Cut out 20 smaller pastry shapes, using a small round or star cutter and place them on top of the apple sauce. Lightly press the rims together and brush the pastry with egg. Bake for 15–20 minutes or until golden brown. Let them cool on a wire rack and dust with icing sugar to serve, if you like.

Mince pies are not part of the Scandinavian Christmas tradition and you cannot buy mincemeat in Scandinavia, so back home in Denmark I started making small apple pies inspired by the spicing in a British mince pie.

You cannot go through December in Denmark without these doughnuts (*æbleskiver*). Most people buy them ready-made, which is a real shame because those are really boring! This is my family recipe, and they are the best. Adding prunes is an old tradition, but they can be left out if you prefer, or replaced by a piece of apple pushed into each doughnut instead.

Doughnuts and spiced white gløgg

<<<<<<<<<<<<<<<<<<<<<<<<<<<<<<<<<<<<<<<<<<<<<<<<<<<<<<

Serves 8

For the doughnuts
40g/1½oz fresh yeast
800ml/3⅓ cups lukewarm
  whole milk
600g/4½ cups plain/all-purpose
  flour
2½ tsp salt
1½ tsp ground cardamom
2 vanilla pods/beans
3 Tbsp caster or granulated
  sugar
4 eggs, separated
150g/⅔ cup butter
200g/7oz prunes, pitted
  (optional)
icing/confectioners' sugar,
  to serve
Raspberry 'Jam' (page 138),
  to serve
For the gløgg
Day 1
300ml/1¼ cups elderflower
  cordial
10 cardamom pods
8 cloves
1 cinnamon stick
Day 2
2 bottles dry white wine
Spiced Syrup (see above)
1 Tbsp caster sugar
200g/1½ cups sultanas/golden
  raisins
100g/⅞ cup flaked/slivered
  almonds
cognac (optional)

Crumble the yeast into the milk in a large bowl and stir to dissolve. In another large bowl, sift together the flour, salt and cardamom. Slit the vanilla pods lengthways, scrape out the seeds with the tip of a sharp knife and add to the dry ingredients with the sugar. Whisk the eggs yolks into the milk mixture. Add the dry ingredients and beat to make a dough. In a separate bowl, whisk the egg whites until stiff, then fold into the dough. Leave to rest for 40 minutes.

Heat an æbleskiver pan (see photo, left) over a medium heat. Put a little butter in each indentation and, when it has melted, pour in some of the batter. Place half a prune (if using) in each and cook for 3–5 minutes or until golden underneath, then turn the doughnuts over. Continue frying for about 4–5 minutes or until golden, then remove. Repeat with the remaining batter. Dust with icing sugar and serve immediately with raspberry jam.

Gløgg

<<<<<<<<<<<<<<<<<<<<<<<<<<<<<<<<<<<<<<<<<<<<<<<<<<<<<<

Day 1
For the syrup, place the elderflower cordial and spices in a saucepan. Pour in 200ml/⅞ cup water. Gently bring to the boil, then reduce the heat and simmer for 30 minutes. Cover and leave overnight. Strain the syrup to remove the spices.

Day 2
The next day, heat the wine, syrup and sugar in a big pot until almost boiling, then reduce the heat to low, add the sultanas and almonds and simmer for 5 minutes. If using cognac, splosh in a generous measure just before serving. Serve in glasses, giving each guest a teaspoon to catch the sultanas and almonds.

Basics

Buttermilk butter

◇◇

Makes about 250g/9oz

200g/⅞ cup soft butter
75–100ml/5–7 Tbsp buttermilk,
  not too cold
sea salt flakes

Cream the butter in an electric mixer, then pour in the buttermilk little by little, still beating. Season with the salt flakes to taste.

Keep the butter at room temperature before serving but, if you refrigerate it to keep overnight, or if it is a very hot day, take it out of the refrigerator 30 minutes before serving to allow it to return to room temperature.

Fried onions

◇◇

Makes 2 handfuls

2 onions
2–3 Tbsp plain/all-purpose flour
pinch of salt
500ml/2 cups oil for deep-frying

Peel the onions and slice into 5mm/¼in thick rings. In a bowl, gently mix them with the flour and salt. Transfer to a plate to lose any excess flour. Heat the oil in a deep, heavy-based saucepan until hot enough for an onion ring dropped in to start sizzling right away. Deep-fry the onions in small batches until light golden. Do not cook them for too long, otherwise they will become bitter. Remove from the oil with a slotted spoon, and drain on kitchen paper.

Basic Danish pastry dough

<><><><><><><><><><><><><><><><><><><><><><><><><><><><><><><><><><><><><>

**Makes enough for
20–24 pastries**

25g/generous ¾oz fresh yeast
1 egg, lightly beaten
½ tsp salt
1 Tbsp caster or granulated
  sugar
325g/2¾ cups 00 grade (tipo
  00) flour, plus more to dust
300g/1⅓ cups cold butter,
  in thin slices

Crumble the yeast into 150ml/⅝ cup lukewarm water, stir to dissolve, then add the egg, salt and sugar. Stir in the flour and knead the dough with your hands until it is even and light. Put it in a bowl, cover with cling film/plastic wrap and let it rest in the refrigerator for about 15 minutes.

Roll out the dough on a lightly floured work surface into a rough 45cm/18in square. Arrange a square of butter in the centre at a 45° angle to the corners of the dough, so it forms a smaller diamond inside the pastry square. Fold the corners of the pastry over the butter to encase it fully and seal the joins well. Roll out the dough again carefully, this time into a rectangle, making sure that it does not crack and expose the butter.

Then fold a short end one-third over into the centre, and the other short end over that: you are folding the rectangle into 3, as you would a business letter. Wrap in cling film and rest once more in the refrigerator for 15 minutes.

Repeat this rolling and folding procedure 3 times in total, remembering to let the dough rest for 15 minutes in the refrigerator between each. Now the dough is ready to make any 'Danish'.

◇◇◇◇◇◇◇◇◇◇◇◇◇◇◇◇◇◇◇◇◇◇◇

The great thing about *wienerbrød* is that it all comes from the same basic pastry dough, so, when you master that, you can make all the different versions. The pastry is not hard to make but it takes time and, as with a lot of things in life, the more you do it the better you will become.

◇◇◇◇◇◇◇◇◇◇◇◇◇◇◇◇◇◇◇◇◇◇◇

If you heat chocolate without controlling the crystals in the cocoa butter through 'tempering', you risk it losing its shine and having stripes when it dries. If you want a shiny finish with a nice snap, temper the chocolate!

Tempered chocolate

◇◇

This is the easy way to temper chocolate, though you will need a sugar thermometer.

Chop the best dark chocolate (at least 60% cocoa solids) finely, take two-thirds of it and place in a heatproof bowl fitted over a pan of very gently simmering water. Make sure the bowl does not touch the water and that the water does not get too hot.

When the chocolate has melted and reached 50°C/122°F, add the remaining chopped chocolate and mix until all the chocolate has melted. Heat very gently until the melted chocolate reaches a temperature of about 31°C/88°F. Now the chocolate is tempered and ready to be used.

Homemade marzipan

<><><><><><><><><><><><><><><><><><><><><><><><><><><><><><><><><><><><>

Makes 600g/1lb 5oz

500g/1lb 2oz almonds (either
  skin on, or blanched for pure
  white marzipan)
100g/¾ cup icing/confectioners'
  sugar, plus more to dust

Whizz the almonds in a food processor until they become a paste. Add the icing sugar, whizz again, then add 50ml/3¼ Tbsp water and whizz for a final time.

Take the marzipan out of the food processor and knead it on a work surface dusted with icing sugar. Now it is ready to be used for cakes and sweets. It will keep for up to 2 weeks, wrapped in cling film/plastic wrap in the refrigerator.

Choux pastry

<><><><><><><><><><><><><><><><><><><><><><><><><><><><><><><><><><><><>

**Makes enough for about
  16 choux buns**

100g/scant ½ cup butter
100g/¾ cup plain/all-purpose
  flour
½ tsp caster or granulated
  sugar
pinch of salt
3 eggs, lightly beaten

Put the butter in a saucepan with 200ml/⅞ cup water and bring to the boil. Meanwhile, sift the flour, sugar and salt into a bowl. Add the flour to the saucepan and stir with a wooden spoon until a firm, smooth paste is formed. Beat until it comes away from the edges of the pan and forms a ball, then cook for 3–4 minutes. Now remove from the heat and leave to cool for 10 minutes.

Add the eggs to the dough a little at a time, beating well after each addition, until the mixture is smooth and glossy. You may not need all the egg.

The dough is now ready to be used.

Make sure to buy good-quality marzipan if you can't make your own.
The way to know it's good is that it will contain at least 55–60% almonds.

Raspberry 'jam'

◇◇

Makes about 400g/14oz
———
300g/10½oz frozen raspberries
100g/½ cup caster or
   granulated sugar

Place the frozen raspberries in a small heavy-based saucepan and bring to the boil, stirring all the time. Now add the sugar and let the jam simmer for 20 minutes. Leave to cool. It should be very thick.

Gooseberry and vanilla 'jam'

◇◇

Makes about 2.5kg/5½lb
———
2 vanilla pods/beans
2kg/4½lb green gooseberries,
   topped and tailed
800g/4 cups caster or
   granulated sugar

Halve the vanilla pods lengthways and place in a pan with the gooseberries and sugar. Bring to the boil, then reduce the heat and simmer for 30 minutes.

Pour the hot jam into hot, sterilised jars (see below) and seal tightly. When cool, store in the refrigerator or a very cold, dark room.

Sterilising jars and bottles

◇◇

I sterilise glass jars and bottles by pouring boiling water into each, closing them tightly and shaking them well. Pour out the water and they are ready to use.

Jam in Denmark means a runny, fresh confection, made in the summer on the day the berries are picked. They are just ripe berries boiled with sugar in a very short time. Make these at least the day before you need them!

Index

Publishing Director Sarah Lavelle
Commissioning Editor Céline Hughes
Designer Gemma Hayden
Photographer Columbus Leth
Illustrator Debbie Powell
Production Controller Sinead Hering
Production Director Vincent Smith

Published in 2019 by Quadrille,
an imprint of Hardie Grant Publishing

Quadrille
52–54 Southwark Street
London SE1 1UN
quadrille.com·

Recipes in the book have been
previously published by Quadrille
in *Scandinavian Baking* (2014) and
Scandinavian Comfort Food (2016).

Reprinted in 2019
10 9 8 7 6 5 4 3 2

Text © Trine Hahnemann 2014, 2016
   and 2019
Photography © Columbus Leth 2014,
   2016 and 2019
Design © Quadrille 2019
Illustration © Debbie Powell 2019

ISBN 978-1-78713-407-2

Printed in China